The Art
of the Novel

BOOKS BY MILAN KUNDERA

The Joke

Laughable Loves

Life Is Elsewhere

Farewell Waltz
(EARLIER TRANSLATION: *The Farewell Party*)

The Book of Laughter and Forgetting

The Unbearable Lightness of Being

Immortality

Slowness

Identity

Ignorance

Jacques and His Master (PLAY)

The Art of the Novel (ESSAY)

Testaments Betrayed (ESSAY)

MILAN KUNDERA

The Art
of the Novel

Translated from the French by Linda Asher

HarperPerennial
A Division of HarperCollins*Publishers*

This book was first published in French in 1986 under the title *L'Art du roman* by Editions Gallimard. A hardcover edition of the English translation was originally published in 1988 by Grove Press. It is hereby reprinted by arrangement with Grove Press, a division of Wheatland Corporation.

First Perennial Library edition published 1988.

First HarperPerennial edition published 1993.
Revised edition published 2000.

Library of Congress Cataloging-in-Publication Data
Kundera, Milan.
   [Art du roman. English]
   The art of the novel / Milan Kundera.—Rev. ed.
     p. cm.
   Rev. ed. of the translation from the French by Linda Asher.
   ISBN 0-06-093294-5
   1. Fiction—History and criticism.   2. Kundera, Milan—Technique.
3. Fiction—Technique. I. Title.
PN3453.K8613   2000
809.3—dc21   99-35317

02 03 04 ❖/RRD 10 9 8 7 6 5 4 3 2

CONTENTS

The world of theories is not my world. These are simply the reflections of a practitioner. Every novelist's work contains an explicit vision of the history of the novel, an idea of what the novel is. It is the idea of the novel inherent in my novels that I give voice to here.

The seven pieces comprising this book were written, published, or spoken before an audience between 1979 and 1985. Despite their separate births, I conceived them all with the idea of eventually bringing them together. That came about in 1986. Since then, the book has often been reprinted in France, giving me the opportunity to return to it several times in order to better it. The resulting changes, along with a few minor refinements of her translation by the translator, have been incorporated in this printing.

M. K., January 2000

PART ONE

The Depreciated Legacy of Cervantes

1.

In 1935, three years before his death, Edmund Husserl gave his celebrated lectures in Vienna and Prague on the crisis of European humanity. For Husserl, the adjective "European" meant the spiritual identity that extends beyond geographical Europe (to America, for instance) and that was born with ancient Greek philosophy. In his view, this philosophy, for the first time in history, apprehended the world (the world as a whole) as a question to be answered. It interrogated the world not in order to satisfy this or that practical need but because "the passion to know had seized mankind."

The crisis Husserl spoke of seemed to him so profound that he wondered whether Europe was still able to survive it. The roots of the crisis lay for him at the beginning of the Modern Era, in Galileo and Descartes, in the one-sided nature of the European sciences, which reduced the world to a mere object of technical and mechanical investigation and put the concrete world of life, *die Lebenswelt* as he called it, beyond their horizon.

The rise of the sciences propelled man into the tunnels of the specialized disciplines. The more he advanced in knowledge, the less clearly could he see either the world as a whole or his own self, and he plunged further into what Husserl's pupil Heidegger called, in a beautiful and almost magical phrase, "the forgetting of being."

Once elevated by Descartes to "master and proprietor of nature," man has now become a mere thing to the forces (of technology, of politics, of history) that bypass him, surpass him, possess him. To those forces, man's concrete being, his "world of life" (*die Lebenswelt*), has neither value nor interest: it is eclipsed, forgotten from the start.

2.

Yet I think it would be naive to take the severity of this view of the Modern Era as a mere condemnation. I would say rather that the two great philosophers laid bare the ambiguity of this epoch, which is decline and progress at the same time and which, like all that is human, carries the seed of its end in its beginning. To my mind, this ambiguity does not diminish the last four centuries of European culture, to which I feel all the more attached as I am not a philosopher but a novelist. Indeed, for me, the founder of the Modern Era is not only Descartes but also Cervantes.

Perhaps it is Cervantes whom the two phenomenologists neglected to take into consideration in their judgment of the Modern Era. By that I mean: If it is true that philosophy and science have forgotten about man's being, it emerges all the more plainly that with Cervantes a great European art took shape that is nothing other than the investigation of this forgotten being.

Indeed, all the great existential themes Heidegger analyzes in *Being and Time*—considering them to have been neglected by all earlier European philosophy— had been unveiled, displayed, illuminated by four centuries of the European novel. In its own way, through its own logic, the novel discovered the vari- ous dimensions of existence one by one: with Cervan- tes and his contemporaries, it inquires into the nature of adventure; with Richardson, it begins to examine "what happens inside," to unmask the secret life of the feelings; with Balzac, it discovers man's rooted- ness in history; with Flaubert, it explores the *terra* pre- viously *incognita* of the everyday; with Tolstoy, it focuses on the intrusion of the irrational into human behavior and decisions. It probes time: the elusive past with Proust, the elusive present with Joyce. With Thomas Mann, it examines the role of the myths from the remote past that control our present actions. Et cetera, et cetera.

The novel has accompanied man uninterruptedly and faithfully since the beginning of the Modern Era. It was then that the "passion to know," which Husserl considered the essence of European spirituality, seized the novel and led it to scrutinize man's con- crete life and protect it against "the forgetting of being"; to hold "the world of life" under a permanent light. That is the sense in which I understand and share Hermann Broch's insistence in repeating: The sole *raison d'être* of a novel is to discover what only the novel can discover. A novel that does not discover a hitherto unknown segment of existence is immoral. Knowledge is the novel's only morality.

I would also add: The novel is Europe's creation; its discoveries, though made in various languages, belong to the whole of Europe. The *sequence of discoveries* (not the sum of what was written) is what constitutes the history of the European novel. It is only in such a supranational context that the value of a work (that is to say, the import of its discovery) can be fully seen and understood.

3.

As God slowly departed from the seat whence he had directed the universe and its order of values, distinguished good from evil, and endowed each thing with meaning, Don Quixote set forth from his house into a world he could no longer recognize. In the absence of the Supreme Judge, the world suddenly appeared in its fearsome ambiguity; the single divine Truth decomposed into myriad relative truths parceled out by men. Thus was born the world of the Modern Era, and with it the novel, the image and model of that world.

To take, with Descartes, the *thinking self* as the basis of everything, and thus to face the universe alone, is to adopt an attitude that Hegel was right to call heroic.

To take, with Cervantes, the world as ambiguity, to

be obliged to face not a single absolute truth but a welter of contradictory truths (truths embodied in *imaginary selves* called characters), to have as one's only certainty the *wisdom of uncertainty*, requires no less courage.

What does Cervantes's great novel mean? Much has been written on the question. Some see in it a rationalist critique of Don Quixote's hazy idealism. Others see it as a celebration of that same idealism. Both interpretations are mistaken because they both seek at the novel's core not an inquiry but a moral position.

Man desires a world where good and evil can be clearly distinguished, for he has an innate and irrepressible desire to judge before he understands. Religions and ideologies are founded on this desire. They can cope with the novel only by translating its language and relativity and ambiguity into their own apodictic and dogmatic discourse. They require that someone be right: either Anna Karenina is the victim of a narrow-minded tyrant, or Karenin is the victim of an immoral woman; either K. is an innocent man crushed by an unjust Court, or the Court represents divine justice and K. is guilty.

This "either-or" encapsulates an inability to tolerate the essential relativity of things human, an inability to look squarely at the absence of the Supreme Judge. This inability makes the novel's wisdom (the wisdom of uncertainty) hard to accept and understand.

4.

Don Quixote set off into a world that opened wide before him. He could go out freely and come home as he pleased. The early European novels are journeys through an apparently unlimited world. The opening of *Jacques le Fataliste* comes upon the two heroes in mid-journey; we don't know where they've come from or where they're going. They exist in a time without beginning or end, in a space without frontiers, in the midst of a Europe whose future will never end.

Half a century after Diderot, in Balzac, the distant horizon has disappeared like a landscape behind those modern structures, the social institutions: the police, the law, the world of money and crime, the army, the State. In Balzac's world, time no longer idles happily by as it does for Cervantes and Diderot. It has set forth on the train called History. The train is easy to board, hard to leave. But it isn't at all fearsome yet, it even has its appeal; it promises adventure to every passenger, and with it fame and fortune.

Later still, for Emma Bovary, the horizon shrinks to the point of seeming a barrier. Adventure lies beyond it, and the longing becomes intolerable. Within the monotony of the quotidian, dreams and daydreams take on importance. The lost infinity of the outside world is replaced by the infinity of the soul. The great illusion of the irreplaceable uniqueness of the individual—one of Europe's finest illusions—blossoms forth.

But the dream of the soul's infinity loses its magic when History (or what remains of it: the suprahuman force of an omnipotent society) takes hold of man. History no longer promises him fame and fortune; it barely promises him a land-surveyor's job. In the face of the Court or the Castle, what can K. do? Not much. Can't he at least dream as Emma Bovary used to do? No, the situation's trap is too terrible, and like a vacuum cleaner it sucks up all his thoughts and feelings: all he can think of is his trial, his surveying job. The infinity of the soul—if it ever existed—has become a nearly useless appendage.

5.

The path of the novel emerges as a parallel history of the Modern Era. As I look back over it, it seems strangely short and limited. Isn't that Don Quixote himself, after a three-hundred-year journey, returning to the village disguised as a land-surveyor? Once he had set out to seek adventures of his own choosing, but now in the village below the Castle he has no choice, the adventure is *imposed on him:* a petty squabble with the administration over a mistake in his file. So what, after three centuries, has happened to adventure, the first great theme of the novel? Has it become its own parody? What does that mean? That the path of the novel winds up in a paradox?

Yes, so it would seem. And that is by no means the only paradox. *The Good Soldier Schweik* is perhaps the last great popular novel. Isn't it astonishing that this comic novel is also a war novel, whose action unfolds in the army and at the front? What has happened to war and its horrors if they've become laughing matters?

In Homer and in Tolstoy, war had a perfectly comprehensible meaning: people fought for Helen or for Russia. Schweik and his companions go to the front without knowing why and, what is even more shocking, without caring to know.

What, then, is the motor of war if not Helen or country? Sheer force that wills to assert itself as force? The "will to will" that Heidegger later wrote about? Yet hasn't that been behind all wars since the beginning of time? Yes, of course. But this time, in Hasek, it does not try to hide behind even the slightest reasonable argument. No one believes in the drivel of propaganda, not even those who manufacture it. Force is naked here, as naked as in Kafka's novels. Indeed, the Court has nothing to gain from executing K., nor has the Castle from tormenting the Land-Surveyor. Why did Germany, why does Russia today want to dominate the world? To be richer? Happier? Not at all. The aggressiveness of force is thoroughly disinterested; unmotivated; it wills only its own will; it is pure irrationality.

Kafka and Hasek thus bring us face to face with this enormous paradox: In the course of the Modern Era, Cartesian rationality has corroded, one after the other, all the values inherited from the Middle Ages. But just when reason wins a total victory, pure irrationality (force willing only its will) seizes the world stage, because there is no longer any generally accepted value system to block its path.

This paradox, masterfully illuminated in Hermann Broch's *The Sleepwalkers,* is one of those I like to call *terminal*. There are others. For example: The Modern Era has nurtured a dream in which mankind, divided into its separate civilizations, would someday come together in unity and everlasting peace. Today, the history of the planet has finally become one indivisible whole, but it is war, ambulant and everlasting war, that embodies and guarantees this long-desired unity of mankind. Unity of mankind means: No escape for anyone anywhere.

6.

Husserl's lectures on the European crisis and on the possible disappearance of European mankind were his philosophical testament. He gave those lectures in two capitals of Central Europe. This coincidence has a deep meaning: for it was in that selfsame Central Europe that, for the first time in its modern history, the West could see the death of the West, or, more exactly, the amputation of a part of itself, when Warsaw, Budapest, and Prague were swallowed up by the Russian empire. This calamity was engendered by the First World War, which, unleashed by the Hapsburg empire, led to the end of that empire and unbalanced forever an enfeebled Europe.

The time was past when man had only the monster

of his own soul to grapple with, the peaceful time of Joyce and Proust. In the novels of Kafka, Hasek, Musil, Broch, the monster comes from outside and is called History; it no longer has anything to do with the train the adventurers used to ride; it is impersonal, uncontrollable, incalculable, incomprehensible—and it is inescapable. This was the moment (just after the First World War) when the pleiad of great Central European novelists saw, felt, grasped the *terminal paradoxes* of the Modern Era.

But it would be wrong to read their novels as social and political prophecies, as if they were anticipations of Orwell! What Orwell tells us could have been said just as well (or even much better) in an essay or pamphlet. On the contrary, these novelists discover "what only the novel can discover": they demonstrate how, under the conditions of the "terminal paradoxes," all existential categories suddenly change their meaning: What is *adventure* if a K.'s freedom of action is completely illusory? What is *future* if the intellectuals of *The Man Without Qualities* have not the slightest inkling of the war that will sweep their lives away the next day? What is *crime* if Broch's Huguenau not only does not regret but actually forgets the murder he has committed? And if the only great comic novel of the period, Hasek's *Schweik*, uses war as its setting, then what has happened to the *comic*? Where is the difference between *public* and *private* if K., even in bed with a woman, is never without the two emissaries of the Castle? And in that case, what is *solitude*? A burden, a misery, a curse, as some would have us believe, or on the contrary, a supremely precious value in the process of being crushed by the ubiquitous collectivity?

The periods of the novel's history are very long (they have nothing to do with the hectic shifts of fashion) and are characterized by the particular aspect of being on which the novel concentrates. Thus the potential of Flaubert's discovery of the quotidian was only fully developed seventy years later, in James Joyce's gigantic work. The period inaugurated seventy years ago by the pleiad of Central European novelists (the period of *terminal paradoxes*) seems to me far from finished.

7.

The death of the novel has been much discussed for a long time: notably by the Futurists, by the Surrealists, by nearly all the avant-gardes. They saw the novel dropping off the road of progress, yielding to a radically new future and an art bearing no resemblance to what had existed before. The novel was to be buried in the name of historical justice, like poverty, the ruling classes, obsolete cars, or top hats.

But if Cervantes is the founder of the Modern Era, then the end of his legacy ought to signify more than a mere stage in the history of literary forms; it would herald the end of the Modern Era. That is why the blissful smile that accompanies those obituaries of the novel strikes me as frivolous. Frivolous because I have already seen and lived through the death of the novel, a violent death (inflicted by bans, censorship, and ideological pressure), in the world where I spent much of my life and which is usually called totalitarian. At that time it became utterly clear that the novel was mortal; as mortal as the West of the Modern Era. As a model of this Western world, grounded in the relativity and ambiguity of things human, the novel is incompatible with the totalitarian universe. This incompatibility is deeper than the one that separates a dissident from an apparatchik, or a human-rights campaigner from a torturer, because it is not only political or moral but *ontological*. By which I mean: The world of one single Truth and the relative, ambiguous world of the novel are molded of entirely different substances. Totalitarian Truth excludes relativity, doubt, questioning; it can never accommodate what I would call the *spirit of the novel.*

But aren't there hundreds and thousands of novels published in huge editions and widely read in Communist Russia? Certainly; but these novels add nothing to the conquest of being. They discover no new segment of existence; they only confirm what has already been said; furthermore: in confirming what everyone says (what everyone must say), they fulfill their purpose, their glory, their usefulness to that society. By discovering nothing, they fail to participate in the *sequence of discoveries* that for me constitutes the history of the novel; they place themselves *outside* that history, or, if you like: they are *novels that come after the history of the novel.*

About half a century ago the history of the novel came to a halt in the empire of Russian Communism.

That is an event of huge importance, given the greatness of the Russian novel from Gogol to Bely. Thus the death of the novel is not just a fanciful idea. It has already happened. And we now know *how* the novel dies: it's not that it disappears; its history stops: after that comes nothing but a period of repetition in which the novel keeps duplicating its form, emptied of its spirit. Its death occurs quietly, unnoticed, and no one is outraged.

8.

But hasn't the novel come to the end of the road by its own internal logic? Hasn't it already mined all its possibilities, all its knowledge, and all its forms? I've heard the history of the novel compared to a seam of coal long since exhausted. But isn't it more like a cemetery of missed opportunities, of unheard appeals? There are four appeals to which I am especially responsive.

The appeal of play: Laurence Sterne's *Tristram Shandy* and Denis Diderot's *Jacques le Fataliste* are for me the two greatest novelistic works of the eighteenth century, two novels conceived as grand games. They reach heights of playfulness, of lightness, never scaled before or since. Afterward, the novel got itself tied to the imperative of verisimilitude, to realistic settings, to chronological order. It abandoned the possibilities opened up by these two masterpieces, which could have led to a different development of the novel (yes, it's possible to imagine a whole other history of the European novel . . .).

The appeal of dream: The slumbering imagination of the nineteenth century was abruptly awakened by Franz Kafka, who achieved what the Surrealists later called for but never themselves really accomplished: the fusion of dream and reality. This enormous contribution is less the final step in a historical development than an unexpected opening that shows that the novel is a place where the imagination can explode as in a dream, and that the novel can break free of the seemingly inescapable imperative of verisimilitude.

The appeal of thought: Musil and Broch brought a sovereign and radiant intelligence to bear on the novel. Not to transform the novel into philosophy, but to marshal around the story all the means—rational and irrational, narrative and contemplative—that could illuminate man's being; could make of the novel the supreme intellectual synthesis. Is their achievement the completion of the novel's history, or is it instead the invitation to a long journey?

The appeal of time: The period of *terminal paradoxes* incites the novelist to broaden the time issue beyond the Proustian problem of personal memory to the enigma of collective time, the time of Europe, Europe looking back on its own past, weighing up its history like an old man seeing his whole life in a single moment. Whence the desire to overstep the temporal limits of an individual life, to which the novel had hitherto been confined, and to insert in its space several historical periods (Aragon and Fuentes have already tried this).

But I don't want to predict the future paths of the novel, which I cannot know; all I mean to say is this: If the novel should really disappear, it will do so not because it has exhausted its powers but because it exists in a world grown alien to it.

9.

The unification of the planet's history, that humanist dream which God has spitefully allowed to come true, has been accompanied by a process of dizzying reduction. True, the termites of reduction have always gnawed away at life: even the greatest love ends up as a skeleton of feeble memories. But the character of modern society hideously exacerbates this curse: it reduces man's life to its social function; the history of a people to a small set of events that are themselves reduced to a tendentious interpretation; social life is reduced to political struggle, and that in turn to the confrontation of just two great global powers. Man is caught in a veritable *whirlpool of reduction* where Husserl's "world of life" is fatally obscured and being is forgotten.

Now, if the novel's *raison d'être* is to keep "the world of life" under a permanent light and to protect us from "the forgetting of being," is it not more than ever necessary today that the novel should exist?

Yes, so it seems to me. But alas, the novel too is ravaged by the termites of reduction, which reduce not only the meaning of the world but also the meaning of works of art. Like all of culture, the novel is more and more in the hands of the mass media; as agents of the unification of the planet's history, the media amplify and channel the reduction process; they distribute throughout the world the same simplifications and stereotypes easily acceptable by the greatest number, by everyone, by all mankind. And it doesn't much matter that different political interests appear in the various organs of the media. Behind these surface differences reigns a common spirit. You have only to glance at American or European political weeklies, of the left or the right: they all have the same view of life, reflected in the same ordering of the table of contents, under the same headings, in the same journalistic phrasing, the same vocabulary, and the same style, in the same artistic tastes, and in the same ranking of things they deem important or insignificant. This common spirit of the mass media, camouflaged by political diversity, is the spirit of our time. And this spirit seems to me contrary to the spirit of the novel.

The novel's spirit is the spirit of complexity. Every novel says to the reader: "Things are not as simple as you think." That is the novel's eternal truth, but it grows steadily harder to hear amid the din of easy, quick answers that come faster than the question and block it off. In the spirit of our time, it's either Anna or Karenin who is right, and the ancient wisdom of Cervantes, telling us about the difficulty of knowing and the elusiveness of truth, seems cumbersome and useless.

The novel's spirit is the spirit of continuity: each

work is an answer to preceding ones, each work contains all the previous experience of the novel. But the spirit of our time is firmly focused on a present that is so expansive and profuse that it shoves the past off our horizon and reduces time to the present moment only. Within this system the novel is no longer a *work* (a thing made to last, to connect the past with the future) but one current event among many, a gesture with no tomorrow.

10.

Does this mean that, "in a world grown alien to it," the novel will disappear? That it will leave Europe to founder in "the forgetting of being"? That nothing will be left but the endless babble of graphomaniacs, nothing but *novels that come after the history of the novel*? I don't know. I merely believe I know that the novel cannot live in peace with the spirit of our time: if it is to go on discovering the undiscovered, to go on "progressing" as novel, it can do so only against the progress of the world.

The avant-garde saw things differently; it was possessed by an ambition to be in harmony with the future. It is true, avant-garde artists did create works that were courageous, difficult, provocative, ridiculed, but they did so in the conviction that "the spirit of the time" was with them and would soon prove them right.

Once upon a time I too thought that the future was

the only competent judge of our works and actions. Later on I understood that chasing after the future is the worst conformism of all, a craven flattery of the mighty. For the future is always mightier than the present. It will pass judgment on us, of course. And without any competence.

But if the future is not a value for me, then to what am I attached? To God? Country? The people? The individual?

My answer is as ridiculous as it is sincere: I am attached to nothing but the depreciated legacy of Cervantes.

PART TWO

Dialogue on the
Art of the Novel

Christian Salmon: I'd like to discuss the aesthetic of your novels. But where shall we begin?

M.K.: With this assertion: My novels are not psychological. More precisely: They lie outside the aesthetic of the novel normally termed psychological.

C.S.: But aren't all novels necessarily psychological? That is, concerned with the enigma of the psyche?

M.K.: Let's be more precise: All novels, of every age, are concerned with the enigma of the self. As soon as you create an imaginary being, a character, you are automatically confronted by the question: What is the self? How can the self be grasped? It is one of those fundamental questions on which the novel, as novel, is based. By the various responses to that question, if you wanted, you could distinguish different tendencies, and perhaps different periods, in the history of the novel. The psychological approach wasn't even known to the first European storytellers. Boccaccio simply tells us about actions and adventures. Still, behind all those amusing tales, we can make out this conviction: It is through action that man steps forth from the repetitive universe of the everyday where each person resembles every other person; it is through action that he distinguishes himself from others and becomes an individual. Dante said as much: "In any act, the primary intention of the one who acts is to reveal his own image." At the outset, action is thus seen as the self-portrait of the one who acts. Four centuries after Boccaccio, Diderot is more skeptical: his Jacques le Fataliste seduces his friend's girl, he gets happily drunk, his father wallops him, a regiment marches by, out of spite he signs up, in his first battle he gets a bullet in the knee, and he limps till the day of his death. He thought he was starting an amorous adventure, and instead he was setting forth toward his infirmity. He could never recognize himself in his action. Between the act and himself, a chasm opens. Man hopes to reveal his own image through his act, but that image bears no resemblance to him. The paradoxical nature of action is one of the novel's great discoveries. But if the self is not to be grasped through action, then where and how are we to grasp it? So the time came when the novel, in its quest for the self, was forced to turn away from the visible world of action and examine instead the invisible interior life. In the middle of the eighteenth century, Richardson discovers the form of the epistolary novel in which the characters confess their thoughts and their feelings.

C.S.: The birth of the psychological novel?

M.K.: The term is, of course, inexact and approximate. Let's avoid it and use a periphrasis: Richardson set the novel on its way to the exploration of man's interior life. We know his great successors: the Goethe of *Werther*, Laclos, Constant, then Stendhal and the other writers of his century. The apogee of that evolution is to be found, it seems to me, in Proust and in Joyce. Joyce analyzes something still more ungraspable than Proust's "lost time": the present moment. There would seem to be nothing more obvious, more tangible and palpable, than the present moment. And yet it eludes us completely. All the sadness of life lies in that fact. In the course of a single second, our senses of sight, of hearing, of smell, register (knowingly or not) a swarm of events, and a parade of sensations and ideas passes through our heads. Each instant represents a little universe, irrevocably forgotten in the next instant. Now, Joyce's great microscope manages to stop, to seize, that fleeting instant and make us see it. But the quest for the self ends, yet again, in a paradox: The more powerful the lens of the microscope observing the self, the more the self and its uniqueness elude us; beneath the great Joycean lens that breaks the soul down into atoms, we are all alike. But if the self and its uniqueness cannot be grasped in man's interior life, then where and how can we grasp it?

C.S.: Can it be grasped at all?

M.K.: Of course not. The quest for the self has always ended, and always will end, in a paradoxical dissatisfaction. I don't say defeat. For the novel cannot breach the limits of its own possibilities, and bringing those limits to light is already an immense discovery, an immense triumph of cognition. Nonetheless, after reaching the depth involved in the detailed exploration of the self's interior life, the great novelists began, consciously and unconsciously, to seek a new orientation. We often hear of the holy trinity of the modern novel: Proust, Joyce, Kafka. In my view, that trinity does not exist. In my own personal history of the novel, it is Kafka who provided this new orientation: a post-Proustian orientation. His way of conceiving the self is totally unexpected. What is it that defines K. as a unique being? Neither his physical appearance (we know nothing about that), nor his biography (we don't know it), nor his name (he has none), nor his memories, his predilections, his complexes. His behavior? His field of action is lamentably limited. His thoughts? Yes, Kafka unceasingly traces K.'s reflections, but these are bent exclusively on the current situation: What should be done then and there, in the immediate circumstances? Go to the interrogation or evade it? Obey the priest's summons or not? All of K.'s interior life is absorbed by the situation he finds himself trapped in, and nothing that might refer beyond that situation (K.'s memories, his metaphysical reflections, his notions about other people) is revealed to us. For Proust, a man's interior universe comprises a miracle, an infinity that never ceases to amaze us. But that is not what amazes Kafka. He does not ask what internal motivations determine man's behavior. He asks a question that is radically different: What possibilities remain for man in a world where the external determinants have become so overpowering that internal impulses no longer carry weight? Indeed, how could it have changed K.'s destiny and attitude if he had had homosexual inclinations or an unhappy love affair behind him? In no way.

C.S.: That's what you say in *The Unbearable Lightness of Being:* "The novel is not the author's confession; it is an investigation of human life in the trap the world has become." But what does that mean, "trap"?

M.K.: That life is a trap we've always known: we are

born without having asked to be, locked in a body we never chose, and destined to die. On the other hand, the wideness of the world used to provide a constant possibility of escape. A soldier could desert from the army and start another life in a neighboring country. Suddenly, in our century, the world is closing around us. The decisive event in that transformation of the world into a trap was surely the 1914 war, called (and for the first time in history) a world war. Wrongly "world." It involved only Europe, and not *all* of Europe at that. But the adjective "world" expresses all the more eloquently the sense of horror before the fact that, henceforward, nothing that occurs on the planet will be a merely local matter, that all catastrophes concern the entire world, and that consequently we are more and more determined by external conditions, by situations that no one can escape and that more and more make us resemble one another.

But understand me: If I locate myself outside the so-called psychological novel, that does not mean that I wish to deprive my characters of an interior life. It means only that there are other enigmas, other questions that my novels pursue primarily. Nor does it mean I object to novels that are fascinated by psychology. In fact, the change in the situation since Proust makes me nostalgic. With Proust, an enormous beauty began to move slowly out of our reach. Forever and irretrievably. Gombrowicz had an idea as comical as it is ingenious: The weight of our self, he said, depends on the size of the population on the planet. Thus Democritus represented a four-hundred-millionth of humanity; Brahms a billionth;

Gombrowicz himself a two-billionth. By that calculation, the weight of the Proustian infinity—the weight of a self, or a self's interior life—becomes lighter and lighter. And in that race toward lightness, we have crossed a fateful boundary.

C.S.: "The unbearable lightness" of the self is your obsession, beginning with your earliest writings. I'm thinking of *Laughable Loves*—for example, the story "Eduard and God." After his first night of love with the young Alice, Eduard is overcome by a strange malaise, one that is decisive for him: he looks at his girl and thinks "that her ideas were in fact only a *veneer* on her destiny, and her destiny only a veneer on her body; he saw her as an accidental conjunction of a body, ideas, and a life's course, an inorganic structure, arbitrary and unstable." And again in another story, "The Hitchhiking Game," in the final paragraphs of the tale, the girl is so upset by her uncertain hold on her identity that she sobs, "I'm me, I'm me, I'm me . . ."

M.K.: In *The Unbearable Lightness of Being*, Tereza is staring at herself in the mirror. She wonders what would happen if her nose were to grow a millimeter longer each day. How much time would it take for her face to become unrecognizable? And if her face no longer looked like Tereza, would Tereza still be Tereza? Where does the self begin and end? You see: Not wonder at the immeasurable infinity of the soul; rather, wonder at the uncertain nature of the self and of its identity.

C.S.: There is a complete absence of interior monologue in your novels.

M.K.: Joyce set a microphone within Bloom's head. Thanks to the fantastic espionage of interior monologue, we have learned an enormous amount about what we are. But, myself, I cannot use that microphone.

C.S.: In *Ulysses*, interior monologue pervades the entire novel; it is the ground of its construction, the dominant process. Could we say that in your work, philosophical meditation plays that role?

M.K.: I find the word "philosophical" inappropriate. Philosophy develops its thought in an abstract realm, without characters, without situations.

C.S.: You begin *The Unbearable Lightness of Being* by reflecting on Nietzsche's eternal return. What's that but a philosophical idea developed abstractly, without characters, without situations?

M.K.: Not at all! That reflection introduces directly, from the very first line of the novel, the fundamental situation of a character—Tomas; it sets out his problem: the lightness of existence in a world where there is no eternal return. You see, we've finally come back to our question: What lies beyond the so-called psychological novel? Or, put another way: What is the nonpsychological means to apprehend the self? To apprehend the self in my novels means to grasp the essence of its existential problem. To grasp its *existential code*. As I was writing *The Unbearable Lightness of Being*, I realized that the code of this or that character is made up of certain key words. For Tereza: body, soul, vertigo, weakness, idyll, Paradise. For Tomas: lightness, weight. In the part called "Words Misunderstood," I examine the existential codes of Franz and Sabina by analyzing a number of words: woman, fidelity, betrayal, music, darkness, light, parades, beauty, country, cemetery, strength. Each of these words has a different meaning in the other person's existential code. Of course, the existential code is not examined *in abstracto;* it reveals itself progressively in the action, in the situations. Take *Life Is Elsewhere,* the third part: The hero, the shy Jaromil, is still a virgin. One day, he is out walking with a girl who suddenly lays her head on his shoulder. He is overcome with happiness and even physically aroused. I pause over that mini-event and note: "The greatest happiness Jaromil had experienced up to this point in his life was having a girl's head on his shoulder." And from that I try to grasp Jaromil's erotic nature: "A girl's head meant more to him than a girl's body." Which does not mean, I make clear, that he was indifferent to the body, but "he didn't long for the nakedness of a girl's body; he longed for a girl's face lighted by the nakedness of her body. He didn't long to possess a girl's body; he longed to possess the face of a girl who would yield her body to him as proof of her love." I try to give a name to that attitude. I choose the word "tenderness." And I examine the word: Just what is tenderness? I arrive at successive answers: "Tenderness comes into being at the moment when life propels a man to the threshold of adulthood, and he anxiously realizes all the advantages of childhood which he had not appreciated as a child." And then: "Tenderness is the fear instilled by adulthood." And then a further definition: Tenderness is the creation of "a tiny artificial space in which it is mutually agreed that each will treat the other like a child." You see, I don't show you what happens inside Jaromil's head; rather, I show what happens inside my own: I observe my Jaromil for a long while, and I try, step by step, to get to the heart of his attitude, in order to understand it, name it, grasp it.

In *The Unbearable Lightness of Being*, Tereza lives with Tomas, but her love requires a mobilization of all her strength, and suddenly she can't go on, she longs to retreat "down below," to where she came from. And I ask myself: What is happening with her? And this is the answer I find: She is overcome by vertigo. But what is vertigo? I look for a definition and I say: "A heady, insuperable longing to fall." But immediately I correct myself, I sharpen the definition: Vertigo is "the intoxication of the weak. Aware of his weakness, a man decides to give in rather than stand up to it. He is drunk with weakness, wishes to grow even weaker, wishes to fall down in the middle of the main square in front of everybody, wishes to be down, lower than down." Vertigo is one of the keys to understanding Tereza. It's not the key to understanding you or me. And yet both of us know that sort of vertigo at least as a possibility for us, one of the possibilities of existence. I had to invent Tereza, an "experimental self," to understand that possibility, to understand vertigo.

But it isn't merely particular situations that are thus interrogated; the whole novel is nothing but one long interrogation. Meditative interrogation (interrogative meditation) is the basis on which all my novels are constructed. Look at *Life Is Elsewhere.* The original title of that novel was "The Lyrical Age." I changed it at the last minute under pressure from friends who found it insipid and distasteful. I was foolish to give in to them. Indeed, I think it's a very good thing to name a novel for its main category. *The Joke. The Book of Laughter and Forgetting. The Unbearable Lightness of Being.* Even *Laughable Loves.* That title should not be taken in the sense of "amusing love stories." The idea of love is always associated with seriousness. But the category "laughable love" is love stripped of seriousness. A critical notion for modern man. But to return to *Life Is Elsewhere.* That novel rests on certain questions: What is the lyrical attitude? How is youth a lyrical age? What is the meaning of the triad: lyricism/revolution/youth? And what is it to be a poet? I remember having begun that novel with this working hypothesis, a definition I set down in my notebook: "The poet is a young man whose mother leads him to display himself to a world he cannot enter." You see, that definition is neither sociological nor aesthetic nor psychological.

C.S.: It's phenomenological.

M.K.: The adjective isn't bad, but I make it a rule not to use it. I'm too fearful of the professors for whom art is only a derivative of philosophical and theoretical trends. The novel dealt with the unconscious before Freud, the class struggle before Marx, it practiced phenomenology (the investigation of the essence of human situations) before the phenomenologists. What superb "phenomenological descriptions" in Proust, who never even knew a phenomenologist!

C.S.: Let's summarize. There are several means of grasping the self. First, through action. Next, through the interior life. As for yourself, you declare: The self is determined by the essence of its existential problem. This view has a number of consequences for your work. For example, your insistence on understanding the essence of situations seems to you to render all descriptive techniques obsolete. You say almost nothing about the physical appearance of your characters. And since the investigation of psychological motives interests you less than the analysis of situations, you are also very parsimonious about your characters' past. Doesn't the overly abstract nature of your narration risk making your characters less lifelike?

M.K.: Try asking the same question of Kafka and Musil. In fact, it was asked of Musil. Even some highly cultivated minds complained that he was not a true novelist. Walter Benjamin admired his intelligence but not his art. Edouard Roditi found his characters lifeless and suggested he take Proust as his model: How alive and real Madame Verdurin is, he says, compared with Diotima! Indeed, the long tradition of psychological realism has created some nearly inviolable standards: (1) A writer must give the maximum amount of information about a character: about his physical appearance, his way of speaking and behaving; (2) he must let the reader know a character's past, because that is where all the motives for his present behavior are located; and (3) the character must have complete independence; that is to say, the author with his own considerations must disappear so as not to disturb the reader, who wants to give himself over to illusion and take fiction for reality. Now, Musil broke that old contract between the novel and the reader. And so did other writers along with him. What do we know about the physical appearance of Esch, Broch's greatest character? Nothing. Except that he has big teeth. What do we know about K.'s childhood, or Schweik's? And neither Musil nor Broch nor Gombrowicz felt the least discomfort at being present as a mind in his novels. A character is not a simulation of a living being. It is an imaginary being. An experimental self. In that way the novel reconnects with its beginnings. Don Quixote is practically unthinkable as a living being. And yet, in our memory, what character is more alive? Understand me, I don't mean to scorn the reader and his desire, as naive as it is legitimate, to be carried away by the novel's imaginary world and to confuse it occasionally with reality. But I don't see that the technique of psychological realism is indispensable for that. I first read *The Castle* when I was fourteen years old. At that same period I admired an ice hockey player who lived near us. I imagined K. as looking like him. I still see him that way today. What I mean is that the reader's imagination automatically completes the writer's. Is Tomas dark or fair? Was his father rich or poor? Choose for yourself!

C.S.: But you don't always follow that rule: in *The Unbearable Lightness of Being*, Tomas has virtually no past, but Tereza is presented not merely with her own childhood but her mother's as well!

M.K.: In the novel, you will find this sentence: "Her entire life was a mere continuation of her mother's, much as the course of a ball on the billiard table is the continuation of the player's arm movement." If I talk about the mother, then, it's not in order to set down data on Tereza, but because the mother is her main theme, because Tereza is the "continuation of her mother" and suffers from it. We also know that she has small breasts with areolae that are "very large, very dark circles around her nipples," as if they were "painted by a primitivist of poor-man's pornography"; that information is indispensable because her body is another of Tereza's main themes. By contrast, where Tomas, her husband, is concerned, I tell nothing about his childhood, nothing about his father, his mother, his family. And his body, as well as his face, remains completely unknown to us because the essence of his existential problem is rooted in other themes. That lack of information does not make him the less "living." Because making a character "alive" means: getting to the bottom of his existential problem. Which in turn means: getting to the bottom of some situations, some motifs, even some words that shape him. Nothing more.

C.S.: Your conception of the novel, then, could be defined as a poetic meditation on existence. Yet your novels have not always been understood in that way. They contain many political events that have provoked sociological, historical, or ideological interpretations. How do you reconcile your interest in social history with your conviction that a novel examines primarily the enigma of existence?

M.K.: Heidegger characterizes existence by an extremely well-known formulation: *in-der-Welt-sein,* being-in-the-world. Man does not relate to the world as subject to object, as eye to painting; not even as actor to stage set. Man and the world are bound together like the snail to its shell: the world is part of man, it is his dimension, and as the world changes, existence (*in-der-Welt-sein*) changes as well. Since Balzac, the world of our being has a historical nature, and characters' lives unfold in a realm of time marked by dates. The novel can never rid itself of that legacy from Balzac. Even Gombrowicz, who invents fantastical, improbable stories, who violates all the rules of verisimilitude, cannot escape it. His novels take place in a time that has a date and is thoroughly historical. But two things should not be confused: there is on the one hand the novel that examines *the historical dimension of human existence,* and on the other the novel that is *the illustration of a historical situation,* the description of a society at a given moment, a novelized historiography. You're familiar with all those novels about the French Revolution, about Marie Antoinette, or about the year 1914, about collectivization in the USSR (for or against it), or about the year 1984; all those are popularizations that translate non-novelistic knowledge into the language of the novel. Well, I'll never tire of repeating: The novel's sole *raison d'être* is to say what only the novel can say.

C.S.: But what specifically can the novel say about history? Or, what is your way of treating history?

M.K.: Here are some of my own principles. First: All historical circumstances I treat with the greatest economy. I behave toward history like the stage designer who constructs an abstract set out of the few items indispensable to the action.

Second principle: Of the historical circumstances, I keep only those that create a revelatory existential situation for my characters. Example: In *The Joke*, Ludvik sees all his friends and colleagues raise their hands to vote, with utter ease, his exclusion from the university and thus to topple his life. He is certain that they would, if necessary, have voted with the same ease to hang him. Whence his definition of man: a being capable in any situation of consigning his neighbor to death. Ludvik's fundamental anthropological experience thus has historical roots, but the description of the history itself (the role of the Party, the political bases of terror, the organization of social institutions, etc.) does not interest me, and you will not find it in the novel.

Third principle: Historiography writes the history of society, not of man. That is why the historical events my novels talk about are often forgotten by historiography. Example: In the years that followed the 1968 Russian invasion of Czechoslovakia, the reign of terror against the public was preceded by officially organized massacres of dogs. An episode totally forgotten and without importance for a historian, for a political scientist, but of the utmost anthropological significance! By this one episode alone I suggested the historical climate of *Farewell Waltz*. Another example: At the crucial point of *Life Is Elsewhere*, history intervenes in the form of an inelegant and shabby pair of undershorts; there were no others to be had at the time; faced with the loveliest erotic occasion of his life, Jaromil, for fear of looking ridiculous in his shorts, dares not undress and takes flight instead. Inelegance! Another historical circumstance forgotten, and yet how important for the person obliged to live under a Communist regime.

But it is the fourth principle that goes furthest: Not only must historical circumstance create a new existential situation for a character in a novel, but history *itself* must be understood and analyzed as an existential situation. Example: In *The Unbearable Lightness of Being*, Alexander Dubcek—after being arrested by the Russian army, kidnapped, jailed, threatened, forced to negotiate with Brezhnev—returns to Prague. He speaks over the radio, but he cannot speak, he gasps for breath, in mid-sentence he makes long, awful pauses. What this historical episode reveals for me (an episode, by the way, completely forgotten because, two hours later, the radio technicians were made to cut the painful pauses out of his speech) is *weakness*. Weakness as a very general category of existence: "Any man confronted with superior strength is weak, even if he has an athletic body like Dubcek's." Tereza cannot bear the spectacle of that weakness, which repels and humiliates her, and she chooses to emigrate. But in the face of Tomas's infidelities, she is like Dubcek faced with Brezhnev: defenseless and weak. And you know already what vertigo is: intoxication with one's own weakness, the insuperable desire to fall. Tereza abruptly understands that "she belonged among the weak, in the camp of the weak, in the country of the weak, and that she had to be faithful to them precisely because they were weak and gasped for breath in the middle of sentences." And, intoxicated with weakness, she leaves Tomas and returns to Prague, back to the "city of the weak." Here the historical situation is not a background, a stage set before which human situations unfold; it is itself a human situation, a growing existential situation.

Similarly, the Prague Spring in *The Book of Laughter and Forgetting* is not described in its politico-historico-social aspect but as a fundamental existential situation: man (a generation of men) acts (makes a revolution), but his action slips out of control, ceases to obey him (the revolution rages, kills, destroys); he thereupon does his utmost to recapture and subdue that disobedient act (a new generation starts an opposition, reformist movement), but in vain. Once out of our hands, the act can never be recaptured.

C.S.: Which recalls the situation of Jacques le Fataliste that you discussed at the beginning.

M.K.: But this time, it's a matter of a collective, historical situation.

C.S.: To understand your novels, is it important to know the history of Czechoslovakia?

M.K.: No. Whatever needs to be known of it the novel itself tells.

C.S.: Reading novels doesn't presume any historical knowledge?

M.K.: We have the history of Europe. From the year 1000 up to our time, that has been a single common experience. We are part of that, and our every action, individual or national, only reveals its crucial significance when set in that context. I can understand *Don*

Quixote without knowing the history of Spain. I cannot understand it without some idea, however general, of Europe's historical experience—of its age of chivalry, for instance, of courtly love, of the shift from the Middle Ages to the Modern Era.

C.S.: In *Life Is Elsewhere*, each phase of Jaromil's life is seen against fragments from the biographies of Rimbaud, Keats, Lermontov, and so on. The May Day Parade in Prague is merged with the May 1968 student demonstrations in Paris. Thus you create for your hero a huge setting that encompasses the whole of Europe. Still, your novel takes place in Prague. It culminates in the Communist putsch in 1948.

M.K.: For me, it is a novel of the European revolution as such, in its condensed form.

C.S.: European revolution—that putsch? An import, moreover, from Moscow?

M.K.: However inauthentic it was, that putsch was experienced as a revolution. With all its rhetoric, its illusions, reflexes, actions, crimes, I see it today as a parody condensation of the European revolutionary tradition. As the continuation and grotesque fulfillment of the era of European revolutions. Just as the hero of that book, Jaromil—the "continuation" of Victor Hugo and Rimbaud—is the grotesque fulfillment of European poetry. Jaroslav, in *The Joke*, continues the age-old history of popular art at a time when that art is vanishing. Doctor Havel, in *Laughable Loves*, is a Don Juan at a time when Don Juanism is no longer possible. Franz, in *The Unbearable Lightness of Being*, is the last melancholy echo of the Grand March of the European left. And Tereza, in her obscure village in

Bohemia, is withdrawing not only from all the public life of her country but also "from the road along which mankind, 'the master and proprietor of nature,' marches onward." All these characters fulfill not only their personal histories but also the suprapersonal history of the European experience.

C.S.: Which means that your novels take place in the last act of the Modern Era, which you call the "period of terminal paradoxes."

M.K.: If you like. But let's head off any misunderstanding. When I wrote Havel's story in *Laughable Loves*, I had no intention of describing a Don Juan in a time when the adventure of Don Juanism was ending. I was writing a story I found funny. That's all. All these reflections on terminal paradoxes, et cetera, did not precede my novels but proceeded from them. It was while I was writing *The Unbearable Lightness of Being* that—inspired by my characters, all of whom are in some fashion withdrawing from the world—I thought of the fate of Descartes's famous formulation: man as "master and proprietor of nature." Having brought off miracles in science and technology, this "master and proprietor" is suddenly realizing that he owns nothing and is master neither of nature (it is vanishing, little by little, from the planet), nor of History (it has escaped him), nor of himself (he is led by the irrational forces of his soul). But if God is gone and man is no longer master, then who is master? The planet is moving through the void without any master. There it is, the unbearable lightness of being.

C.S.: Still, isn't it an egocentric mirage to see the present time as the special moment, the most important of all—that is, the moment of the end? How many times already has Europe believed it was living through its end, its apocalypse!

M.K.: Among all those terminal paradoxes, there is also the one of the end itself. When a phenomenon announces in advance its imminent disappearance, many of us hear the news and perhaps even regret it. But when the mortal agony draws to a close, we are already looking elsewhere. The death becomes invisible. It's some time now since the river, the nightingale, the paths through the fields have disappeared from man's mind. No one needs them now. When nature disappears from the planet tomorrow, who will notice? Where are the successors to Octavio Paz, to René Char? Where are the great poets now? Have they vanished, or have their voices only grown inaudible? In any case, an immense change in our Europe, which was hitherto unthinkable without its poets. But if man has lost the need for poetry, will he notice when poetry disappears? The end is not an apocalyptic explosion. There may be nothing so quiet as the end.

C.S.: Granted. But if one thing is ending, we might suppose that something else is beginning.

M.K.: Certainly.

C.S.: But what is it that's beginning? That doesn't show in your novels. Whence the doubt: Aren't you seeing only half of our historical situation?

M.K.: It's possible, but that isn't so very grave. Indeed, it's important to understand what a novel is. A historian tells you about events that have taken place. By contrast, Raskolnikov's crime never saw the light of day. A novel examines not reality but existence. And existence is not what has occurred, existence is the realm of human possibilities, everything that man can become, everything he's capable of. Novelists draw up *the map of existence* by discovering this or that human possibility. But again, to exist means: "being-in-the-world." Thus *both* the character *and* his world must be understood as *possibilities*. In Kafka, all that is clear: the Kafkan world does not resemble any known reality, it is an *extreme and unrealized possibility* of the human world. It's true that this possibility shows faintly behind our own real world and seems to prefigure our future. That's why people speak of Kafka's prophetic dimension. But even if his novels had nothing prophetic about them, they would not lose their value, because they grasp one possibility of existence (a possibility for man and for his world) and thereby make us see what we are, what we are capable of.

C.S.: But your own novels are located in a world that is thoroughly real!

M.K.: Remember Broch's *The Sleepwalkers,* a trilogy that encompasses thirty years of European history. For Broch, that history is clearly defined as a perpetual *disintegration of values.* The characters are locked into this process as in a cage and must find a way of living that suits the progressive disappearance of common values. Broch was, of course, convinced of the correctness of his historical judgment—that is, convinced that the possibility of the world he was describing was a possibility come true. But let's try to imagine that he was mistaken and that parallel to this process of disintegration another process was at work, a positive development that Broch was unable to see. Would that make any difference to the value of *The Sleepwalkers*? No. Because the process of disintegration of values is an indisputable possibility of the human world. To understand man flung into the vortex of that process, to understand his gestures, his attitudes—that's all that matters. Broch discovered an unknown new territory of existence. Territory of existence means: possibility of existence. Whether or not that possibility becomes a reality is secondary.

C.S.: The period of terminal paradoxes where your novels are located must be considered, then, not as reality but as possibility?

M.K.: A possibility for Europe. A possible vision of Europe. A possible situation for man.

C.S.: But if you are trying to grasp a possibility rather than a reality, why take seriously the image you offer of Prague, for example, and of the events that occurred there?

M.K.: If the writer considers a historical situation a fresh and revealing possibility of the human world, he will want to describe it as it is. Still, fidelity to historical reality is a secondary matter as regards the value of the novel. The novelist is neither historian nor prophet: he is an explorer of existence.

PART THREE

Notes Inspired by "The Sleepwalkers"

Composition

A trilogy composed of three novels: *Pasenow, or Romanticism; Esch, or Anarchy; Huguenau, or Realism* (in German, *Sachlichkeit*). The story of each novel takes place fifteen years after that of the preceding one: 1888; 1903; 1918. None of the novels is bound to another by causal connection: each has its own circle of characters, and its construction is unlike that of the two others.

It is true that Pasenow (protagonist of the first novel) and Esch (protagonist of the second) meet on the stage of the third, and that Bertrand (a character in the first novel) plays a role in the second. However, the story that Bertrand lives through in the first novel (along with Pasenow, Ruzena, Elisabeth) is completely absent from the second novel, and when Pasenow appears in the third novel he carries with him not the slightest memory of his youth (which is treated in the first novel).

There is thus a radical difference between *The Sleepwalkers* and the other great twentieth-century "frescoes" (those of Proust, Musil, Thomas Mann, etc.): In Broch, it is continuity neither of action nor of biography (a character's or a family's) that provides the unity of the whole. It is something else, something less apparent, less apprehensible, something hidden: the continuity of one *theme* (that of man facing the process of a disintegration of values).

Possibilities

What are the possibilities for man in the trap the world has become?

To answer this, one must first have a certain idea of what the world is. One must have an ontological hypothesis about it.

The world according to Kafka: the bureaucratized universe. The office not merely as one kind of social phenomenon among many but as the essence of the world.

Here lies the resemblance (a curious, unexpected resemblance) between Kafka the hermetic and Hasek the popular. In *The Good Soldier Schweik*, Hasek does not describe the army (in the manner of a realist, a social critic) as a milieu of Austro-Hungarian society but as the modern version of the world. Like Kafka's Court, Hasek's army is nothing but an immense bureaucratic institution, an army-administration in which the old military virtues (courage, cunning, skill) no longer matter.

Hasek's military bureaucrats are stupid; the pedantic and absurd logic of Kafka's bureaucrats is also devoid of wisdom. In Kafka, stupidity is swathed in a mantle of mystery and takes on the quality of metaphysical parable. It intimidates. Joseph K. does his utmost to make some sense of its actions, its unintelligible words. For, terrible as it is to be condemned to death, it is intolerable to be condemned for nothing, to be a martyr to senselessness. Despite his innocence, K. therefore consents to his guilt and searches for his offense. In the last chapter, he shields his two executioners from the eyes of the municipal police (who might have saved him) and, moments before his death, reproaches himself for not having the strength to plunge the knife into his own chest and spare them the dirty job.

Schweik is just the opposite of K. He mimics the world around him (the world of stupidity) in so perfectly systematic a fashion that no one can tell if he is truly imbecilic or not. He adapts so easily (and with such delight!) to the reigning order not because he sees some sense in it but because he sees it has none at all. He amuses himself, he amuses other people, and by his extravagant conformism, he turns the world into one enormous joke.

(Those of us who have experienced the totalitarian Communist version of the modern world know that these two attitudes—seemingly artificial, literary, exaggerated—are only too real; we've lived in the realm bounded on one side by K.'s possibility, on the other by Schweik's; which is to say: in the realm where one pole is the identification with power, to the point where the victim develops solidarity with his own executioner, and the other pole the nonacceptance of power through the refusal to take seriously anything at all; which is to say: we have lived in the space between the absolute of the serious—K.—and the absolute of the nonserious—Schweik.)

And what about Broch? What is his ontological hypothesis?

The world is the process of the disintegration of values (values handed down from the Middle Ages), a process that stretches over the four centuries of the Modern Era and is their very essence.

What are man's possibilities in the face of this process?

Broch finds three: the Pasenow possibility, the Esch possibility, the Huguenau possibility.

The Pasenow Possibility

Joachim von Pasenow's brother dies in a duel. The father says: "He died for honor." These words are writ forever in Joachim's memory.

But his friend Bertrand is amazed: How is it possible that in the age of trains and factories, two men can stand stiffly face to face, arms extended, revolvers in hand?

Upon which Joachim thinks: Bertrand has no feeling for honor.

And Bertrand goes on: Sentiments resist the changing times. They are an indestructible underpinning of conservatism. An atavistic residue.

Yes, the sentimental attachment to inherited values, to their atavistic residue, is Joachim von Pasenow's attitude.

Pasenow is introduced by the uniform motif. In earlier times, explains the narrator, the Church, as Supreme Judge, ruled over man. The priest's robes were the mark of supraterrestrial power, whereas the officer's uniform, the magistrate's gown represented the profane. As the magical influence of the Church gradually faded, the uniform replaced the sacerdotal habit and rose to the level of the absolute.

The uniform is that which we do not choose, that which is assigned us; it is the certitude of the universal as against the precariousness of the individual. When the values that were once so solid come under challenge and withdraw, heads bowed, he who cannot live without them (without fidelity, family, country, discipline, without love) buttons himself up in the universality of his uniform as if that uniform were the last shred of the transcendence that could protect him against the cold of a future in which there will be nothing left to respect.

Pasenow's story culminates on his wedding night. His wife, Elisabeth, does not love him. He sees nothing ahead but a future of lovelessness. He lies down beside her without undressing. That "twisted his uniform a little, the coat skirts fell open and revealed the front of his black trousers, but as soon as Joachim noticed, he hastily set things right again and covered the place. He had drawn up his legs, and so as not to touch the coverlet with his glossy boots, he strained to keep his feet on the chair beside the bed."

The Esch Possibility

The values handed down from the time when the Church completely dominated men's lives had long been shaken loose, but for Pasenow their content still seems clear. He has no doubt about what his country is, he knows to whom he should be faithful and who is his God.

In the presence of Esch, values have hidden their

faces. Order, loyalty, sacrifice—he cherishes all these words, but exactly what do they represent? Sacrifice for what? Demand what sort of order? He doesn't know.

If a value has lost its concrete content, what is left of it? A mere empty form; an imperative that goes unheeded and, all the more furious, demands to be heard and obeyed. The less Esch knows what he wants, the more furiously he wants it.

Esch: the fanaticism of the era with no God. Because all values have hidden their faces, anything can be considered a value. Justice, order—Esch seeks them now in the trade union struggle, then in religion; today in police power, tomorrow in the mirage of America, where he dreams of emigrating. He could be a terrorist or a repentant terrorist turning in his comrades, or a party militant or a cult member or a kamikaze prepared to sacrifice his life. All the passions rampaging through the bloody history of our time are taken up, unmasked, diagnosed, and terrifyingly displayed in Esch's modest adventure.

He is discontented at the office where he works, he has a quarrel, he is dismissed. That is how his story begins. He believes that the cause of all the disorder that upsets him is a man named Nentwig, a bookkeeper. God knows why he in particular. In any case, Esch decides to denounce him to the police. Isn't it his duty? Isn't it a service he owes everyone who, like himself, wants law and order?

But one day, in a bar, the unsuspecting Nentwig genially invites him to his table and offers him a drink. Beside himself, Esch tries to remember Nentwig's offense, but "by now it was so bizarrely insubstantial and vague that Esch suddenly saw the absurdity of his project, and with a clumsy gesture, a little ashamed after all, he seized his glass."

For Esch the world divides into the kingdom of Good and the kingdom of Evil, but alas, both Good and Evil are equally impossible to identify (he has only to run into Nentwig and Esch no longer knows who is righteous and who wicked). In the great masquerade that is the world, Bertrand alone bears the stigmata of Evil forever on his face, because his crime is beyond all doubt: he is a homosexual, a disturber of the divine order. At the start of his novel Esch is ready to denounce Nentwig; at the end he mails a letter denouncing Bertrand.

The Huguenau Possibility

Esch denounced Bertrand. Huguenau denounces Esch. Esch did it to save the world. Huguenau does it to save his career.

In a world without shared values, Huguenau, the innocent arriviste, feels perfectly at ease. The absence of moral imperatives is his freedom, his deliverance.

There is a deep significance in the fact that it is he who—without the faintest sense of guilt—murders Esch. For "it is always the adherent of the smaller value system who slays the adherent of the larger system that is breaking up; it is always he, unfortunate wretch, who assumes the role of executioner in the process of value disintegration, and on the day when

53

the trumpets of Judgment sound, it is the man released from all values who becomes the executioner of a world that has pronounced its own sentence."

In Broch's mind, the Modern Era is the bridge that leads from the reign of irrational faith to the reign of the irrational in a world without faith. The figure who appears at the end of that bridge is Huguenau. The cheerful, guilt-free murderer. The end of the Modern Era in its euphoric version.

K., Schweik, Pasenow, Esch, Huguenau: five basic possibilities, five lodestars without which I believe it impossible to draw the existential map of our time.

Under the Skies of the Ages

The planets that wheel in the skies of the Modern Era are reflected, always in a specific configuration, in the individual soul; it is through this configuration that the character's situation and the sense of his being are defined.

Broch speaks of Esch and all at once compares him to Luther. Both belong to the rebel category (Broch analyzes it at length). "Esch is a rebel like Luther." We tend to look for a character's roots in his childhood. Esch's roots (his childhood remains unknown to us) are to be found in another century. Esch's past is Luther.

To understand Pasenow, that man in uniform, Broch had to place him in the midst of the long historical process during which the profane uniform took the place of the priest's habit; immediately he did that, the whole celestial vault of the Modern Era lit up over this paltry officer.

For Broch, a character is conceived not as a uniqueness, immitable and transitory, a miraculous moment fated to disappear, but as a solid bridge erected above time, where Luther and Esch, the past and the present, come together.

It is less in his philosophy of history than in this new way of seeing man (seeing him under the celestial arch of the ages) that Broch in *The Sleepwalkers* prefigures, I think, the future possibilities of the novel.

By Broch's light, I read Thomas Mann's *Doctor Faustus*, a novel that examines not only the life of a composer named Adrian Leverkühn but several centuries of German music along with him. Adrian is not only a composer, he is the composer who brings the history of music to an end (his greatest work is, incidentally, called *The Apocalypse*). And he is not just the last composer, he is also Faust. His gaze fixed on his country's diabolism (he wrote the novel toward the end of the Second World War), Thomas Mann ponders the contract that the mythical doctor—the incarnation of the German spirit—made with the devil. The whole history of his country suddenly looms up as the single adventure of a single character: a single Faust.

By Broch's light, I read Carlos Fuentes's *Terra Nostra*, in which the whole great Hispanic adventure (European and American) is encompassed in a wonderful telescoping, a wonderful oneiric distortion. Fuentes transforms Broch's principle, *Esch is like Luther*, into a still more radical principle: *Esch is*

Luther. He provides us the key to his method: "It takes several lives to make one person." The old mythology of reincarnation materializes in a novelistic technique that makes *Terra Nostra* an immense, strange dream in which history is made and continually traversed by the same characters endlessly reincarnated. The same Ludovico who found a hitherto unknown continent in Mexico turns up several centuries later in Paris, with the same Celestina who centuries earlier was the mistress of Philip II. And so on.

Only at the end (the end of a love, of a life, of an era) does the past suddenly show itself as a whole and take on a brilliantly clear and finished shape. For Broch, the moment of the end is Huguenau; for Mann, Hitler. For Fuentes, it is the mythical frontier between two millennia; seen from that imaginary observatory, history—that European oddity, that smudge on time's pure surface—looks finished already, abandoned, lonely, and suddenly as humble, as touching as some little personal story we'll forget by tomorrow.

Indeed, if Luther is Esch, the history that leads from Luther to Esch is merely the biography of a single person: Martin Luther-Esch. And all of history is merely the story of a few characters (a Faust, a Don Juan, a Don Quixote, a Rastignac, an Esch) who have traversed Europe's centuries together.

Beyond Causality

On Levin's estate, a man and a woman meet—two melancholy, lonely people. They like each other and secretly hope to join their lives together. All they need is the chance to be alone for a moment and say so. Finally one day they find themselves unobserved in a wood where they have come to gather mushrooms. Ill at ease, they are silent, knowing that the moment is upon them and they must not let it slip by. The silence has already lasted rather a long while when the woman suddenly, "involuntarily, reflexively," starts to talk about mushrooms. Then silence again, and the man casts about for a way to declare himself, but instead of speaking of love, "on some unexpected impulse" he too talks about mushrooms. On the way home they go on discussing mushrooms, powerless and desperate, for never, they know it, never will they speak of love.

Back at the house, the man tells himself that he did not declare his love because of the memory of his dead mistress, which he cannot betray. But we know perfectly well: It is a false excuse he invokes only to console himself. Console himself? Yes. Because we can resign ourselves to losing a love for a reason. We would never forgive ourselves for losing it for no reason at all.

This very beautiful little episode is a kind of parable for one of *Anna Karenina*'s great feats: bringing to light the causeless, incalculable, even mysterious aspect of human action.

What is action?—the eternal question of the novel, its constitutive question, so to speak. How is a decision born? How is it transformed into an act, and how do acts connect to make an adventure?

Out of the mysterious and chaotic fabric of life, the

old novelists tried to tease the thread of a limpid rationality; in their view, the rationally accessible motive gives birth to an act, and that act provokes another. An adventure is a luminously causal chain of acts.

Werther loves his friend's wife. He cannot betray his friend, he cannot give up his love, so he kills himself. Suicide with the transparent clarity of a mathematical equation.

But why does Anna Karenina kill herself?

The man who talked about mushrooms instead of love wants to believe that he did so out of loyalty to his vanished mistress. The reasons we might give for Anna's act would be worth just as little. True, people are treating her with contempt, but can she not do the same to them? She is barred from seeing her son, but is that a situation beyond appeal and beyond hope of change? Vronsky is already a little less infatuated, but after all, doesn't he still love her?

Besides, Anna did not come to the station to kill herself. She came to meet Vronsky. She throws herself beneath the train without having taken the decision to do so. It is rather the decision that takes Anna. That overtakes her. Like the man who talked about mushrooms instead of love, Anna acts "on some unexpected impulse." Which does not mean that her act is senseless. But its sense lies outside rationally apprehensible causality. Tolstoy had to use (for the first time in the history of the novel) an almost Joycean interior monologue to reconstruct the subtle fabric of fleeting impulses, transient feelings, fragmentary thoughts, to show us the suicidal journey of Anna's soul.

With Anna, we are far from Werther, and far from Dostoyevsky's Kirilov too. Kirilov kills himself because he is forced to it by very clearly defined interests, carefully delineated intrigues. His act, however mad, is rational, conscious, meditated, premeditated. Kirilov's character is based entirely on his strange philosophy of suicide, and his act is merely the perfectly logical extension of his ideas.

Dostoyevsky grasped the madness of reason stubbornly determined to carry its logic through to the end. The terrain Tolstoy explores is the opposite: he uncovers the intrusions of illogic, of the irrational. That is why I mention him. The reference to Tolstoy places Broch in the context of one of the great explorations of the European novel: the exploration of the role the irrational plays in our decisions, in our lives.

Con-fusions

Pasenow is seeing a Czech whore named Ruzena, but his parents arrange his marriage to a girl of their own milieu: Elisabeth. Pasenow loves her not at all, yet she does attract him. Actually, what attracts him is not Elisabeth herself but all that Elisabeth *represents* for him.

When he goes to see her for the first time, the streets, the gardens, the houses of her neighborhood radiate "a great and insular security"; Elisabeth's house welcomes him with its happy atmosphere of "a safe and gentle existence, filled with friendship" that will someday "give place to love," which in turn will someday "die away into friendship." The value Pasenow desires (the friendly security of a family) presents itself to him before he ever sees the woman who is to become (without her knowledge and against her nature) the bearer of that value.

He sits in the church in his native village and, eyes closed, imagines the Holy Family on a silver cloud with the ineffably beautiful Virgin Mary in its midst. Already as a child he had been carried away by that same image in that same church. At the time he was in love with a Polish servant girl on his father's farm, and in his reverie, he confused her with the Virgin and imagined himself sitting on her lovely knees, the knees of the Virgin turned servant girl. This time, his eyes closed, he sees the Virgin again and, all of a sudden, notices that her hair is blond! Yes, Mary has Elisabeth's hair! He is startled, he is shaken! It seems to him that through the device of this reverie, God himself is telling him that Elisabeth, whom he does not love, is actually his true and only love.

Irrational logic is based on the mechanism of con-fusion: Pasenow has a poor sense of reality; the causes of events escape him; he will never know what lies hidden behind the gazes of other people; yet although it may be disguised, unrecognizable, causeless, the external world is not mute: it speaks to him. It is like Baudelaire's famous poem where "long echoes . . . are confounded," where "the sounds, the scents, the colors correspond": one thing is like another, is confounded with it (Elisabeth is con-

founded with the Virgin), and thus through its like-
ness makes itself clear.

Esch is a lover of the absolute. "We can love only
once" is his motto, and since Frau Hentjen loves him,
according to Esch's logic she must not have loved her
late husband. This means the man misused her and
can only have been a villain. A villain like Bertrand.
For the representatives of evil are interchangeable.
They become con-fused with each other. They are
only different manifestations of the same essence. It is
when Esch glimpses Herr Hentjen's portrait on the
wall that the idea comes to his mind: to go immediately and denounce Bertrand to the police. For if Esch
can strike at Bertrand it will be like wounding Frau
Hentjen's husband—as if he were ridding us, all of us,
of a small share of the common evil.

Forests of Symbols

We must read *The Sleepwalkers* carefully, slowly, lin-
ger over actions as illogical as they are comprehensible, in order to perceive a hidden, subterranean *order*
underlying the decisions of a Pasenow, a Ruzena, an
Esch. These characters are not capable of facing reality as a concrete thing. Before their eyes everything
turns into a symbol (Elisabeth the symbol of familial
serenity, Bertrand the symbol of hell), and it is to
symbols they are reacting when they believe they are
acting upon reality.

Broch shows us that it is the system of con-fusions,
the system of *symbolic thought*, that underlies all

behavior, individual as well as collective. We need only examine our own lives to see how much this irrational system, far more than any reasoned thought, directs our attitudes: a certain man who, with his passion for aquarium fish, evokes some other who in the past caused me some terrible misery will always excite insurmountable mistrust in me . . .

The irrational system rules political life no less: along with the last world war Communist Russia won the war of symbols: it succeeded for at least a half-century in providing the symbols of Good and Evil to that great army of Esches who are as avid for values as they are incapable of discriminating among them. This is why the gulag will never supplant Nazism as a symbol of absolute evil in the European consciousness. This is why people hold massive demonstrations against the war in Vietnam and not against the war in Afghanistan. Vietnam, colonialism, racism, imperialism, fascism, Nazism—all these words correspond like the colors and sounds in Baudelaire's poem, while the Afghanistan war is, so to speak, *symbolically mute*, or at any rate beyond the magic circle of absolute Evil, the geyser of symbols.

I also think of those daily slaughters along the highways, of that death that is as horrible as it is banal and that bears no resemblance to cancer or AIDS because, as the work not of nature but of man, it is an almost voluntary death. How can it be that such a death fails to dumbfound us, to turn our lives upside down, to incite us to vast reforms? No, it does not dumbfound us, because like Pasenow, we have a poor sense of the real, and in the sur-real sphere of symbols, this death in the guise of a handsome car actually represents life; this smiling death is con-fused with modernity, freedom, adventure, just as Elisabeth was con-fused with the Virgin. The death of a man condemned to capital punishment, though infinitely rarer, much more readily draws our attention, rouses passions: confounded with the image of the executioner, it has a symbolic voltage that is far stronger, far darker and more repellent. Et cetera.

Man is a child wandering lost—to cite Baudelaire's poem again—in the "forests of symbols."

(The criterion of maturity: the ability to resist symbols. But mankind grows younger all the time.)

Polyhistoricism

In discussing his novels, Broch rejects the aesthetic of the "psychological" novel in favor of the novel he calls "gnosiological" or "polyhistorical." It seems to me that the second term, especially, is ill-chosen and misleading. It was a compatriot of Broch's, Adalbert Stifter, founding father of Austrian fiction, who created a "polyhistorical novel" in the precise sense of the term when in 1857 (yes, the great year of *Madame Bovary*) he wrote *Der Nachsommer* (*Indian Summer*). The novel is well known, Nietzsche having ranked it among the four great books of German prose. To me it is barely readable: we learn a great deal about geology, botany, zoology, about all the crafts, about painting and architecture, but man and human situations stand way off at the margins of this gigantic instructive encyclopedia. Precisely because of its "polyhistoricism," this novel completely lacks the novel's specificity.

Now, this is not the case with Broch. He pursues "what only the novel can discover." But he knows that the conventional form (grounded exclusively in a character's adventure, and content with a mere narration of that adventure) limits the novel, reduces its cognitive capacities. He also knows that the novel has an extraordinary power of incorporation: whereas neither poetry nor philosophy can incorporate the novel, the novel can incorporate both poetry and philosophy without losing thereby anything of its identity, which is characterized (we need only recall Rabelais and Cervantes) precisely by its tendency to embrace other genres, to absorb philosophical and scientific knowledge. So in Broch's perspective, the word "polyhistorical" means: marshaling all intellectual means and all poetic forms to illuminate "what only the novel can discover": man's being.

This, of course, implies a profound transformation of the novel's form.

The Unachieved

I shall take the liberty of speaking very personally: I like and admire the last novel of *The Sleepwalkers* (*Huguenau, or Realism*), in which the tendency to synthesis and the transformation of form are most advanced, but I also have some reservations:

—the "polyhistorical" purpose demands a technique of ellipsis that Broch has not completely worked out; architectural clarity suffers for it;

—the several elements (verse, narrative, aphorism, reportage, essay) remain more juxtaposed than blended into a true "polyphonic" unity;

—even though it is presented as a text written by one of the characters, the excellent essay on the disintegration of values can readily be taken for the author's own thinking, for the novel's truth, its statement, its thesis, and thus may damage the relativity that is indispensable to novelistic space.

All great works (precisely because they are great) contain something unachieved. Broch is an inspiration to us not only because of what he brought off but also because of what he aimed for and missed. The unachieved in his work can show us the need for (1) a new art of *radical divestment* (which can encompass the complexity of existence in the modern world without losing architectonic clarity); (2) a new art of *novelistic counterpoint* (which can blend philosophy, narrative, and dream into one music); (3) a new art of the *specifically novelistic essay* (which does not claim to bear an apodictic message but remains hypothetical, playful, or ironic).

Modernisms

Of all the great novelists of our time, Broch is, perhaps, the least known. It is not so hard to understand why. He had scarcely completed *The Sleepwalkers* when he saw Hitler in power and German cultural life annihilated; five years later he left Austria for America, where he remained until his death. In such conditions, his work—deprived of its natural audience, deprived of contact with a normal literary life—could no longer play its proper role in its time: gather to itself a community of readers, supporters, and connoisseurs, create a school, influence other writers. Like the work of Musil and Gombrowicz, it was discovered (rediscovered) after a long delay (and after its author's death) by those who, like Broch himself, were possessed by the passion for the new form—in other words, who were "modernist" in orientation. But their modernism did not resemble Broch's. Not that it was later, more advanced; it was different in its roots, in its attitude toward the modern world, in its aesthetic. That difference brought about a certain embarrassment: Broch (like Musil, like Gombrowicz) was seen as a great innovator, but one who did not conform to the current and conventional image of modernism (for in the second half of this century, we must reckon with the modernism of fixed rules, the modernism of the university—establishment modernism, so to speak).

This establishment modernism, for instance, insists on the destruction of the novel form. In Broch's perspective, the possibilities of the novel form are far from being exhausted.

Establishment modernism would have the novel do away with the artifice of character, which it claims is finally nothing but a mask pointlessly hiding the author's face. In Broch's characters, the author's self is undetectable.

Establishment modernism has proscribed the notion of totality—the very word that Broch, by contrast, uses readily to say: In the age of the excessive division of labor, of runaway specialization, the novel is one of the last outposts where man can still maintain connections with life in its entirety.

According to establishment modernism, an impregnable boundary separates the "modern" novel from the "traditional" novel (this "traditional novel" being the basket into which they shovel all the different phases of four centuries of the novel). In Broch's view, the modern novel continues the same quest that has preoccupied all the great novelists since Cervantes.

Behind establishment modernism there is a residue of ingenuous eschatological belief: that one history ends and another (better) one begins, founded on an entirely new basis. In Broch, there is the melancholy awareness of a history drawing to a close in circumstances that are profoundly hostile to the evolution of art and of the novel in particular.

PART FOUR

Dialogue
on the
Art of Composition

Christian Salmon: I'll begin this discussion by quoting from your "Notes Inspired by *The Sleepwalkers*." You say: "All great works (precisely because they are great) contain something unachieved. Broch is an inspiration to us not only because of what he brought off but also because of what he aimed for and missed. The unachieved in his work can show us the need for (1) a new art of *radical divestment* (which can encompass the complexity of existence in the modern world without losing architectonic clarity); (2) a new art of *novelistic counterpoint* (which can blend philosophy, narrative, and dream into one music); (3) a new art of the *specifically novelistic essay* (which does not claim to bear an apodictic message but remains hypothetical, playful, or ironic)." These three points seem to set out your own artistic project. Let's begin with the first. The radical divestment.

M.K.: Encompassing the complexity of existence in the modern world demands a technique of ellipsis, of condensation. Otherwise you fall into the trap of endless length. *The Man Without Qualities* is one of the two or three novels I love most, but don't ask me to admire its enormous unfinished size. Imagine a castle so big that it can't all be seen at once. Imagine a string quartet that goes on for nine hours. There are anthropological limits—the limits of memory, for instance—that ought not to be exceeded. When you reach the end of a book you should still find it possible to remember the beginning. Otherwise the novel loses shape, its "architectonic clarity" is clouded.

C.S.: *The Book of Laughter and Forgetting* is made up of seven parts. If you had treated them less elliptically you could have written seven separate full-length novels.

M.K.: But if I had written seven separate novels, I'd have no hope of "encompassing the complexity of existence in the modern world" in one single book. This is why I see the art of ellipsis as crucial. It insists that we go directly to the heart of things. In that regard, I'm reminded of the composer I've admired passionately since I was a child: Leos Janacek. He is one of the great figures of modern music. At a time when Schoenberg and Stravinsky were still writing works for full orchestra, he had already come to feel that orchestral scores collapse under the weight of superfluous notes. That will to divest was the start of his rebellion. You know, any musical composition involves a good deal of purely technical activity: exposition of a theme, development, variations, polyphonic work that is frequently quite mechanical, filling in the orchestration, transitions, and so on. These days music can be composed by computer, but there was always a kind of computer present in composers' heads: in a pinch, they could write a sonata without a single original idea, simply by following "cybernetically" the rules of composition. Janacek's imperative was: Destroy the "computer"! Harsh juxtapositions instead of transitions, repetition instead of variation, and always head straight for the heart of things: only the note that says something essential has the right to exist. Roughly the same idea applies to the novel: it too is weighed down by "technique," by the conventions that do the author's work for him: present a character, describe a milieu, bring the action into a historical situation, fill time in the characters' lives with superfluous episodes; each shift of scene calls for new exposition, description, explanation. My own imperative is "Janacekian": to rid the novel of the automatism of novelistic technique, of novelistic verbalism; to make it dense.

C.S.: Secondly, you mention a "new art of novelistic counterpoint." You're not entirely satisfied with Broch's work there.

M.K.: Take the third book of *The Sleepwalkers*. It is made up of five purposely heterogeneous "lines": (1) the *novelistic narrative* involving the trilogy's three main characters: Pasenow, Esch, and Huguenau; (2) Hanna Wendling's *short story*; (3) the *reportage* about a military hospital; (4) the *poetic narrative* (partly in verse) about a Salvation Army girl; and (5) the *philosophical essay* (written in technical language) on the disintegration of values. Each of the five lines is magnificent in itself. Still, though they are handled simultaneously, in constant alternation (that is, with a clear "polyphonic" intention), the lines do not come together, do not make an indivisible whole; in other words, the polyphonic intention remains artistically unfulfilled.

C.S.: Doesn't this metaphoric application of the term "polyphony" to literature set up demands a novel could never meet?

M.K.: Polyphony in music is the *simultaneous* presentation of two or more voices (melodic lines) that are perfectly bound together but still keep their relative independence. And polyphony in the novel? First let's set out its opposite: *unilinear* composition. Now, since its very beginnings, the novel has always tried to escape the unilinear, to open rifts in the continuous narration of a story. Cervantes tells the story of Don Quixote's journey, which is quite linear. But as he travels, Quixote meets other characters who tell their own stories. In the first part there are four such. Four rifts that allow us to step outside the novel's linear framework.

C.S.: But that's not polyphony!

M.K.: Because there's no simultaneity to it. To borrow Shklovsky's terminology, these are stories "packed inside" the "box" of the novel. You find that same "box" technique in many seventeenth- and eighteenth-century novels. The nineteenth century developed another method of breaking out of the linear mode, the method that—for want of a better term—we can call polyphonic. *The Possessed.* If you analyze that novel from the purely technical viewpoint, you see that it is made up of three lines evolving simultaneously, each of which, if need be, could make an independent novel: (1) the *ironic* novel of the love between Madame Stavrogin and Stepan Verkhovensky; (2) the *romantic* novel about Nikolai Stavrogin and his amorous relationships; (3) the *political* novel about a revolutionary group. Since all the characters know one another, a subtle storytelling technique easily manages to tie the three lines into an indivisible entity. Now compare that Dostoyevskian polyphony to Broch's. His goes much further. While the three lines in *The Possessed*, though different in *character*, are of the same *genre* (all three are *novelistic*), in Broch the five lines differ radically in genre: novel, short story, reportage, poem, essay. That integration of non-novelistic genres into the polyphony of the novel was Broch's revolutionary innovation.

C.S.: But you say those five lines are not adequately welded together. In fact, Hanna Wendling doesn't know Esch, the Salvation Army girl never learns that Hanna Wendling exists. So no storytelling technique could make a single whole of those five distinct lines that do not meet, do not intersect.

M.K.: They are bound only by a common theme. But to me that thematic unity is perfectly sufficient. The problem of disunity lies elsewhere. To recapitulate: In Broch's work, the five lines evolve simultaneously, without meeting, united by one or several themes. I've described that sort of construction by a term borrowed from musicology: polyphony. You'll see that it's not so farfetched to compare the novel to music. Indeed, one of the fundamental principles of the great polyphonic composers was the *equality of voices*: no one voice should dominate, none should serve as mere accompaniment. Now, what appears to me a failing in the third novel of *The Sleepwalkers* is that the five "voices" are not equal. Line number one (the "novelistic" narrative about Esch and Huguenau) takes up quantitatively more space than the other lines, and most important, it dominates qualitatively too, insofar as it is connected to the two preceding books through Esch and Pasenow. It thus commands greater attention and threatens to relegate the four other "lines" to the role of mere "accompaniment." A second point: Whereas a Bach fugue cannot do without any one of its voices, we can easily imagine the Hanna Wendling short story or the essay on the disintegration of values as separate, freestanding texts whose deletion would cost the novel none of its meaning or intelligibility. Now, to my mind, the conditions *sine qua non* for counterpoint in the novel are: first, the equality of the various "lines," and second, the indivisibility of the whole. I remember the day I finished Part Three of *The Book of Laughter and Forgetting*, the part called "The Angels." I confess I was terrifically proud, convinced I'd discovered a new way of constructing a narrative. That text is composed of the following elements: (1) the anecdote about the two schoolgirls and their levitation; (2) the autobiographical narrative; (3) the critical essay on a feminist book; (4) the fable of the angel and the devil; (5) the narrative about Éluard flying over Prague. None of these elements can exist without the others; they illuminate and explain one another as they explore a single theme, a single question: What is an angel? That question is the one thing that holds them together. Part Six, also called "The Angels," is composed of: (1) the oneiric narrative on Tamina's death; (2) the autobiographical narrative on my father's death; (3) musicological reflections; (4) reflections on the epidemic of forgetting that is ravaging Prague. What is the connection between my father and Tamina undergoing her torment at the hands of the children? To invoke the Lautréamont phrase that the surrealists loved, it is "the encounter of a sewing machine and an umbrella on the dissecting table" of the same theme. Polyphony in the novel is much more poetry than it is technique.

C.S.: In *The Unbearable Lightness of Being,* the counterpoint is less apparent.

M.K.: There the polyphonic quality is most striking in Part Six: the story of Stalin's son, a theological meditation, a political event in Asia, Franz's death in Bangkok, and Tomas's burial in Bohemia are connected by the prevailing question: What is kitsch? That polyphonic passage is the keystone of the whole structure. The whole secret of its architectural balance is right there.

C.S.: What secret?

M.K.: There are two. First: The sixth part is laid out not as a story but as an essay (an essay on kitsch). Fragments of the characters' lives are interpolated into the essay as "examples," as "situations to be analyzed." It is thus—incidentally and briefly—that the reader learns about the ends of Franz's and Sabina's lives, and about the outcome of the relations between Tomas and his son. That ellipsis lightens the structure tremendously. Second, chronologic displacement: The events of Part Six occur after the events of the seventh and last part. Because of that dislocation, the last part, despite its idyllic quality, is flooded with a melancholy that comes from our knowledge of what is to happen.

C.S.: I want to get back to your notes on *The Sleepwalkers.* You've expressed some reservations as to the essay on the disintegration of values. Because of its apodictic tone and technical language, you say, it could be taken as the ideological key to the novel, its "Truth," transforming the whole *Sleepwalkers* trilogy into the mere novelized illustration of one grand idea. That is why you discuss the need for an "art of the specifically novelistic essay."

M.K.: First, one thing is certain: the moment it becomes part of a novel, reflection changes its essence. Outside the novel, we're in the realm of affirmation: everyone is sure of his statements: the politician, the philosopher, the concierge. Within the universe of the novel, however, no one affirms: it is the realm of play and of hypotheses. In the novel, then, reflection is essentially inquiring, hypothetical.

C.S.: But why should a novelist have to forgo the right to express his own philosophy directly and affirmatively in his novel?

M.K.: There is a fundamental difference between the ways philosophers and novelists think. People talk about Chekhov's philosophy, or Kafka's or Musil's, and so on. But just try to draw a coherent philosophy out of their writings! Even when they express their ideas directly, in their notebooks, the ideas are intellectual exercises, paradox games, improvisations, rather than statements of thought.

C.S.: Dostoyevsky is completely affirmative, though, in *Diary of a Writer*.

M.K.: But that is not where we find his best ideas. He is a great thinker only as a novelist. Which is to say that in his characters he is able to create intellectual universes that are extraordinarily rich and original. People tend to find in his characters a projection of his ideas—Shatov, for instance. But Dostoyevsky did his best to guard against that. The first time Shatov appears he is characterized quite cruelly: "He was one of those Russian idealists who, suddenly struck by some immense idea, are left dazzled by it, often forever. They never manage to take control of the idea, they believe in it with a passion, and their whole existence from then on is nothing but an agony writhing under the rock that has nearly crushed them." Thus, even if Dostoyevsky did give Shatov his own ideas, they immediately become relative. The rule holds for Dostoyevsky too: Once it is part of a novel, reflection changes its essence: a dogmatic thought turns hypothetical. This is something philosophers miss when they try to write novels. With one exception—Diderot. His wonderful *Jacques le Fataliste*! Once he crosses the frontier of the novel, the serious encyclopedist turns into a playful thinker: not one sentence of his novel is serious, it's all play. That is why that novel is shamefully undervalued in France. Actually, the book epitomizes everything France has lost and refuses to retrieve. These days the French like ideas better than works. And there is no way to translate *Jacques le Fataliste* into the language of ideas.

C.S.: In *The Joke,* it is Jaroslav who expounds a musicological theory. So the hypothetical nature of the reflection is clear. But there are passages in your novels where you yourself speak out directly.

M.K.: Even if I'm the one speaking, my reflections are connected to a character. I want to think his attitudes, his way of seeing things, in his stead and more deeply than he could do it himself. Part Two of *The*

Unbearable Lightness of Being begins with a long meditation on the interrelations between the body and the soul. Yes, it is the author speaking, but everything he says is valid only within the magnetic field of a character: Tereza. It is Tereza's way of seeing things (though never formulated by her).

C.S.: But often your meditations are not linked to any character: the musicological passages in *The Book of Laughter and Forgetting*, or your thoughts on the death of Stalin's son in *The Unbearable Lightness of Being* . . .

M.K.: That's true. From time to time, I like to intervene directly as author, as myself. In that case, tone is crucial. From the very first word, my thoughts have a tone that is playful, ironic, provocative, experimental, or inquiring. The entire sixth part of *The Unbearable Lightness of Being* ("The Grand March") is an essay on kitsch whose main thesis is: "Kitsch is the absolute denial of shit." All of that meditation on kitsch is vitally important for me, there is a great deal of reflection, experience, study, even passion behind it, but the tone is never serious; it is provocative. That essay is unthinkable outside the novel; it is what I mean by "a specifically novelistic essay."

C.S.: You've spoken of novelistic counterpoint as uniting philosophy, narrative, and dream. Let's consider dream. Oneiric narrative takes up all of Part Two of *Life Is Elsewhere*, it's the basis of Part Six of *The Book of Laughter and Forgetting*, and it runs through *The Unbearable Lightness of Being* by way of Tereza's dreams.

M.K.: Oneiric narrative; let's say, rather: imagination, which, freed from the control of reason and from concern for verisimilitude, ventures into landscapes inaccessible to rational thought. The dream is only the model for the sort of imagination that I consider the greatest discovery of modern art. But how can *uncontrolled* imagination be integrated into the novel, which by definition is supposed to be a *lucid* examination of existence? How can such disparate elements be united? That calls for a real alchemy! The first, I believe, to think of this alchemy was Novalis. He interpolated three dreams into his novel *Heinrich von Ofterdingen*. This was no "realistic" imitation of dreams, of the sort we find in Tolstoy or Mann. It was a great piece of poetry inspired by the "imaginative technique" that is a property of dream. But he wasn't satisfied. Those three dreams, he felt, occurred like islands within the novel. He therefore wanted to go further and write the second volume of the novel as a narration in which dream and reality are bound together, so fully mingled that one cannot be distinguished from the other. But he never wrote that second volume. All we have are some notes describing his aesthetic project. It was realized a hundred and twenty years later, by Franz Kafka, whose novels are that seamless fusion of dream and reality. His novels: that supremely lucid gaze set on the modern world, along with the most unfettered imagination. Above all, Kafka represents an enormous aesthetic revolution. An artistic miracle. For instance, take that amazing chapter in *The Castle* where K. makes love with Frieda for the first time. Or the chapter where he turns a primary school classroom into a bedroom for himself, Frieda, and the two assistants. Before Kafka, such density of imagination was inconceivable. It would of course be ridiculous to imitate him. But like Kafka (and like Novalis), I feel that same desire to bring dream—dream imagination—into the novel. My own way of doing it is not by a "fusion of dream and reality" but by polyphonic confrontation. The "oneiric" narrative is one of the elements in the counterpoint.

C.S.: I'd like to go back to the question of unity in a composition. You've described *The Book of Laughter and Forgetting* as "a novel in variation form." Then is it still a novel?

M.K.: What keeps it from looking like one is that there is no unity of action. It is hard to imagine a novel without that unity. Even the *"nouveau roman"* experiments were grounded in a unity of action (or of inaction). Sterne and Diderot took pleasure in making that unity extremely fragile. Jacques' journey with his Master makes up the smaller part of Diderot's novel; it is a mere comic pretext, a box to hold an array of anecdotes, stories, reflections. Nonetheless, this pretext, this "box," is needed to give the book the feel of a novel, or at least a parody of a novel. However, I believe there is something deeper that guarantees a novel's coherence: thematic unity. And this was always true, by the way. The three narrative lines of *The Possessed* are bound together by storytelling technique, yes, but above all by their common theme: the demons that take possession of man when he loses God. In each of the narrative lines, this theme is considered from a different angle, like a thing reflected in three mirrors. And it's this thing (this abstract thing I call the theme) that gives the novel as a whole an internal coherence, the least visible and the most important kind. In *The Book of Laughter and Forgetting*, the coherence of the whole is created *solely* by the unity of a few themes (and motifs), which are developed in variations. Is it a novel? Yes, to my mind. The novel is a meditation on existence as seen through the medium of imaginary characters.

C.S.: By that broad a definition, we could even call *The Decameron* a novel! All of its stories are connected by the same theme of love and told by the same ten narrators . . .

M.K.: I won't be so provocative as to call *The Decameron* a novel. Still, that book is one of the first efforts in modern Europe to create a large-scale composition in narrative prose, and as such it has a place in the history of the novel *at least* as its source and forerunner. You know, the novel took the particular historical path it took. It could just as easily have taken a completely different one. The novel form is almost boundless freedom. Throughout its history, the novel hasn't taken much advantage of that. It has missed out on that freedom. It has left unexplored many formal possibilities.

C.S.: Still, except for *The Book of Laughter and Forgetting*, your own novels, too, are based on a unity of action, if of a rather loose sort.

M.K.: I've always constructed them on two levels: on the first, I compose the novel's story; over that, I develop the themes. The themes are worked out steadily *within* and *by* the story. Whenever a novel

83

abandons its themes and settles for just telling the story, it goes flat. A theme, on the other hand, can be developed on its own, outside the story. That approach to theme I call *digression*. Digression means: abandoning the story for a moment. All of the reflection on kitsch in *The Unbearable Lightness of Being*, for example, is a digression: I leave off telling the novel's story to go at my theme (kitsch) *directly*. Considered from that viewpoint, digression enhances the discipline of the composition rather than weakening it. I make a distinction between theme and *motif*. Motif is an element of the theme or of the story that appears several times over the course of the novel, always in a different context. For instance, the motif of the Beethoven quartet that moves from Tereza's life into Tomas's thoughts and runs through the various themes as well: the theme of weight, the kitsch theme; or the motif of Sabina's bowler hat, which appears in the Sabina/Tomas, Sabina/Tereza, and Sabina/Franz scenes, and which also illustrates the "words misunderstood" theme.

C.S.: But what exactly do you mean by the word "theme"?

M.K.: A theme is an existential inquiry. And increasingly I realize that such an inquiry is, finally, the examination of certain words, theme-words. Which leads me to emphasize: A novel is based primarily on certain fundamental words. It is like Schoenberg's "tone-row." In *The Book of Laughter and Forgetting*, the "row" goes: forgetting, laughter, angels, *litost*, border. Over the course of the novel, those five principal words are analyzed, studied, defined, redefined, and thus transformed into categories of existence. The novel is built on those few categories the way a house is built on its pillars. The pillars of *The Unbearable Lightness of Being*: weight, lightness, soul, body, the Grand March, shit, kitsch, compassion, vertigo, strength, weakness.

C.S.: Let's talk about the architectonic plan of your novels. All but one of them are divided into seven parts.

M.K.: When I finished *The Joke*, I had no reason to be surprised that it had seven parts. Then I wrote *Life Is Elsewhere*. The book was almost done, and it had six parts. I wasn't satisfied with it. The story seemed flat. Suddenly it occurred to me to put in a story that would take place three years after the hero's death (that is, beyond the time frame of the novel). It became the next-to-last part, the sixth, "The Man in His Forties." Instantly the whole thing seemed right. Later on I realized that this sixth part was a strange parallel to Part Six of *The Joke* ("Kostka"), which also brings an outside person into the novel, opens a secret window through the novel's wall. *Laughable Loves* began as ten stories. When I was putting it in final form, I eliminated three of them and the whole thing became very coherent, in a way that prefigured *The Book of Laughter and Forgetting*: the same themes (especially mystification or hoax) make a single entity out of seven narratives, the fourth and sixth of which are further linked by having the same protagonist, Doctor Havel. In *The Book of Laughter and Forgetting*, too, the fourth and sixth parts are linked by the same character: Tamina. When I wrote *The Unbearable Lightness of Being*, I was determined to break the spell of the number seven. The novel had been conceived as a six-part structure. But the first still seemed shapeless. Finally I realized that it was really two parts, that it was like Siamese twins needing to be separated by delicate surgery. My point is that the seven-part structure doesn't represent some superstitious flirtation with magical numbers, or any rational calculation, but a deep, unconscious, incomprehensible drive, an archetype of form that I cannot escape. My novels are variants of an architecture based on the number seven.

C.S.: How far does this mathematical system go?

M.K.: Take *The Joke*. That novel is narrated by four characters: Ludvik, Jaroslav, Kostka, and Helena. Ludvik's monologue takes up $\frac{2}{3}$ of the book; the monologues of the other three together take up $\frac{1}{3}$ (Jaroslav $\frac{1}{6}$, Kostka $\frac{1}{9}$, Helena $\frac{1}{18}$). That mathematical structure determines what I would call the *lighting of the characters*. Ludvik stands in full light, illuminated from the inside (by his own monologue) and from the outside (the other monologues all sketch his portrait). Jaroslav fills a sixth of the book with his monologue, and his self-portrait is corrected from the outside by Ludvik's monologue. And so on. Each character is lighted at a different intensity and in a different way. Lucie, who is one of the most important characters, has no monologue of her own; she is lighted only from the outside by Ludvik's and Kostka's. The absence of interior lighting gives her a mysterious, elusive quality. She stands, so to speak, behind glass; she cannot be touched.

C.S.: Was the mathematical structure premeditated?

M.K.: No. I discovered all that after *The Joke* was published in Prague, in an article by a Czech literary critic: "The Geometry of *The Joke*." It was a revelation to me. In other words, that "mathematical system" emerges completely naturally as a formal necessity, with no need for any calculation.

C.S.: Is that where your fascination with figures comes from? In every one of your novels, the parts and chapters are numbered.

M.K.: The division of the novel into parts, parts into chapters, chapters into paragraphs—the book's *artic-ulation*—I want to be utterly clear. Each of the seven parts is complete in itself. Each is characterized by its own *narrative mode:* for instance, *Life Is Elsewhere:* Part One: "continuous" narrative (that is, with causal connection between the chapters); Part Two: oneiric narrative; Part Three: "discontinuous" narrative (that is, without causal connection between the chapters); Part Four: polyphonic narrative; Part Five: continuous narrative; Part Six: continuous narrative; Part Seven: polyphonic narrative. Each has its own *perspective* (it is told from the viewpoint of a different imaginary self). Each has its own *length:* the sequence of lengths in *The Joke:* very short; very short; long; short; long; short; long. In *Life Is Elsewhere,* the order is reversed: long; short; long; short; long; very short; very short. I also want each of the chapters to be a small, self-contained entity. This is why I insist that my publishers make the numbers prominent and set the chapters off sharply from one another. (Gallimard's solution is best: each chapter starts on a fresh page.) Let me return to the comparison between the novel and music. A part is a movement. The chapters are measures. These measures may be short or long or quite variable in length. Which brings us to the issue of tempo. Each of the parts in my novels could carry a musical indication: *moderato, presto, adagio,* and so on.

C.S.: So the tempo is determined by the relation between the length of a part and the number of chapters it contains?

M.K.: Look at *Life Is Elsewhere* (the French edition) from that viewpoint:

> Part One: 11 chapters in 71 pages; *moderato*
> Part Two: 14 chapters in 31 pages; *allegretto*
> Part Three: 28 chapters in 82 pages; *allegro*
> Part Four: 25 chapters in 30 pages; *prestissimo*
> Part Five: 11 chapters in 96 pages; *moderato*
> Part Six: 17 chapters in 26 pages; *adagio*
> Part Seven: 23 chapters in 28 pages; *presto*

You see: Part Five has 96 pages and only 11 chapters; a slow, tranquil pace: *moderato.* Part Four has 25 chapters in 30 pages! Which gives a feeling of great speed: *prestissimo.*

C.S.: Part Six has 17 chapters in only 26 pages. If I understand you correctly, that means that it has a fairly rapid tempo. And yet you call it *adagio*!

M.K.: Because the tempo is further determined by something else: the relation between the length of a part and the "real" time of the event it describes. Part Five, "The Poet Is Jealous," represents a whole year of life, whereas Part Six, "The Man in His Forties," deals with only a few hours. Here the brevity of the chapters functions to slow time down, to fix a single great moment. . . . Contrasts in tempi are enormously important to me. They often figure in my earliest idea of a novel, well before I write it. The sixth part of *Life Is Elsewhere, adagio* (a mood of peace and compassion), is followed by Part Seven, *presto* (an agitated, harsh mood). I wanted that final contrast to focus all the emotional power of the novel. Exactly the opposite was the case with *The Unbearable Lightness of Being*. There, from the moment the writing began, I knew that the last part should be *pianissimo* and *adagio* ("Karenin's Smile": a calm, melancholy mood, with few events) and that it would be preceded by one that was *fortissimo, prestissimo* ("The Grand March": a rough, cynical mood, full of events).

C.S.: So a shift in tempo also implies a shift in emotional atmosphere.

M.K.: Another important lesson from music. Like it or not, each passage of a musical composition conveys an emotional expression. The sequence of movements in a symphony or a sonata has always been determined by the unwritten rule of alternating slow and fast movements, which almost automatically meant sad or cheerful movements. Those emotional contrasts soon became an oppressive stereotype that only the great masters could overcome (and even they not always). One particularly well-known example I've always admired is the Chopin sonata whose third movement is a funeral march. What more is there to say after that great farewell? Finish the sonata in the usual way with a lively rondo? Not even Beethoven in his Sonata Opus 26 avoids the stereotype—he follows a funeral march (the third movement there too) with a cheerful finale. But the fourth movement in the Chopin sonata is altogether strange: *pianissimo*, fast and short, with no melody, absolutely unsentimental: a distant gust, a muffled sound that heralds the ultimate forgetting. The juxtaposition of these two movements (sentimental-unsentimental) makes you gasp. It is absolutely original. I mention it to show that to compose a novel is to set different emotional spaces side by side—and that, to me, is the writer's subtlest craft.

C.S.: How exactly has your musical training influenced your writing?

M.K.: Up until the age of twenty-five, I was much more strongly drawn to music than to literature. The best thing I did at that time was a composition for four instruments: piano, viola, clarinet, and percussion. It was almost a caricature preview of the architecture of my novels, whose future existence I didn't even faintly suspect at the time. That Composition for Four Instruments is divided—imagine!—into seven parts. As in my novels, the piece consists of parts that are very heterogeneous in form (jazz; waltz parody; fugue; chorale; etc.), each with different instrumentation (piano and viola; piano solo; viola, clarinet, and percussion; etc.). That formal diversity is balanced by a very strong thematic unity: from start to finish, only two themes (A and B) are elaborated. The three last parts are based on a kind of polyphony that I considered very original at the time, the simultaneous development of the two different and emotionally contradictory themes. For instance, in the last part a recording repeats the third movement (Theme A set as a solemn chorale for clarinet, viola, and piano) at the same time that a variation (in *"barbaro"* style) of Theme B is performed by percussion and trumpet (played by the clarinetist). And another curious parallel: In the sixth part, a new theme, C, makes its only appearance, exactly as Kostka does in *The Joke*, or the man in his forties in *Life Is Elsewhere*. My point, once again, is that the form of a novel, its "mathematical structure," is not a calculated thing; it is an unconscious drive, an obsession. I even used to think that the form that obsessed me was some sort of algebraic definition of my own personality, but one day several years ago, as I was studying Beethoven's Quartet Opus 131, I had to give up that narcissistic and subjective conception of the form. Look:

First movement: slow; fugue form; approximately
   7:30 minutes
Second movement: fast; unclassifiable form; 3:30
Third movement: slow; exposition of a single theme;
   1:00
Fourth movement: slow and fast; theme and variations; 14:00
Fifth movement: very fast; scherzo; 5:30
Sixth movement: very slow; exposition of a single
   theme; 2:00
Seventh movement: fast; sonata form; 6:30

Beethoven is perhaps the greatest architect in all of post-Bach music. He inherited the sonata conceived as a cycle of three or four movements, often in rather random sequence, the first of which (written in sonata form) was always more important than the following movements (written in the form of rondo, minuet, and so on). Beethoven's whole artistic evolution is marked by the determination to transform that assemblage into a true unity. Thus, in his piano sonatas, he gradually shifts the center of gravity from the first to the last movement; he often reduces the sonata to just two parts; he utilizes the same themes in different movements; and so on. But at the same time he tries to bring a maximum of formal diversity into that unity. On several occasions he inserts a large-scale fugue into his sonatas—a very bold move, because a fugue in the midst of a sonata must have seemed at the time as alien as the essay on the disintegration of values in the midst of Broch's novel. The Opus 131 quartet is the pinnacle of architectonic perfection. I want to call your attention to just one detail we've already discussed: the variety of lengths. The third movement is fourteen times shorter than the one that follows it! And it's precisely the two strangely short movements (the third and the sixth) that connect and make a whole of those seven very different parts! If all the parts were about the same length, the unity would fall apart. Why? I can't explain it. But it's so. Seven parts all the same length would be like seven bulky wardrobes set side by side.

C.S.: You've said almost nothing about *Farewell Waltz*.

M.K.: Yet that's the novel dearest to me, in a certain sense. As with *Laughable Loves*, I had more fun, more pleasure writing it than the others. In a different state of mind. It went much faster, too.

C.S.: It has only five parts.

M.K.: It's built on a formal archetype completely different from that of my other novels. It is absolutely homogeneous, without digressions, on a single subject, narrated at the same tempo throughout, very theatrical, stylized, its structure drawn from farce. There is a story in *Laughable Loves* called "Symposium," a parody allusion to Plato's dialogue. Long discussions on love. Now, that piece is constructed just like *Farewell Waltz*: a farce in five acts.

C.S.: What does the word "farce" mean to you?

M.K.: A form that puts enormous stress on plot, with its whole machinery of unforeseen and exaggerated coincidences. Labiche. There is nothing so dubious in a novel now—so ridiculous, so passé, so much in bad taste—as plot, with its farcical excesses. Ever since Flaubert, novelists have tried to do away with plot devices, with the result that the novel is often duller than the dullest life. Yet the early novelists had no such qualms about the improbable. In the first book of *Don Quixote,* there is an inn someplace in the middle of Spain where by pure happenstance everybody turns up: Don Quixote, Sancho Panza, their friends the barber and the priest, then Cardenio, a young man whose fiancée Lucinda had been carried off by a certain Don Fernando, and then in comes Don Fernando's own abandoned fiancée, Dorotea, and later Don Fernando himself with Lucinda, then an officer who has escaped from a Moorish prison, and then his brother who has spent years searching for him, then his daughter Clara, and Clara's lover pursuing her, himself pursued by his father's men ... An accumulation of totally improbable coincidences and encounters. But it would be wrong to see this as naive or clumsy in Cervantes. At the time, novels and readers had not yet signed the verisimilitude pact. They were not looking to simulate reality; they were looking to amuse, amaze, astonish, enchant. They were *playful*, and therein lay their virtuosity. The start of the nineteenth century represents a huge change in the history of the novel. I'd almost say a convulsion. The imperative to imitate reality instantly made Cervantes's inn ludicrous. The twentieth century often rebels against the heritage of the nineteenth. Nonetheless, to simply return to the Cervantean inn is no longer possible. The experience of nineteenth-century realism standing between it and us insures that the game of unlikely coincidences can never again be innocent. It becomes either frankly burlesque, ironic, parodic (*Lafcadio's Adventures* or *Ferdydurke*, for instance), or else fantastic, oneiric. Such is the case with Kafka's first novel, *Amerika*. Read the first chapter, the completely unlikely encounter between Karl Rossmann and his uncle: it is like a nostalgic throwback to the Cervantean inn. Yet in that novel the unlikely (even impossible) circumstances are described in such detail, with such an illusion of the real, that we feel as if we have stepped into a world that, however improbable, is realer than reality. Let's keep this in mind: Kafka stepped into this first "sur-real" universe (his first "fusion of reality and dream") by way of Cervantes's inn, through the door of farce.

C.S.: The word "farce" suggests the idea of entertainment.

M.K.: The great European novel started out as entertainment, and all real novelists are nostalgic for it! And besides, entertainment doesn't preclude seriousness. *Farewell Waltz* asks: Does man deserve to live on this earth, shouldn't the world be freed "from mankind's clutches"? To bring together the extreme gravity of the question and the extreme lightness of the form—that has always been my ambition. And it's not a matter of a purely artistic ambition. The union of a frivolous form and a serious subject lays bare our dramas (those that occur in our beds as well as those we play out on the great stage of history) in all their terrible insignificance.

C.S.: So there are two archetype-forms in your novels: (1) polyphonic composition that brings heterogeneous elements together within an architecture based on the number seven; (2) farcical, homogeneous, theatrical composition that verges on the improbable.

M.K.: I dream constantly of some great unexpected infidelity. But so far I have not managed to break out of my bigamy with those two forms.

PART FIVE

Somewhere Behind

Poets don't invent poems
The poem is somewhere behind
It's been there for a long long time
The poet merely discovers it.

—JAN SKACEL

1.

In one of his books, my friend Josef Skvorecky tells this true story:

An engineer from Prague is invited to a professional conference in London. So he goes, takes part in the proceedings, and returns to Prague. Some hours after his return, sitting in his office, he picks up *Rude Pravo*—the official daily paper of the Party—and reads: A Czech engineer, attending a conference in London, has made a slanderous statement about his socialist homeland to the Western press and has decided to stay in the West.

Illegal emigration combined with a statement of that kind is no trifle. It would be worth twenty years in prison. Our engineer can't believe his eyes. But there's no doubt about it, the article refers to him. His secretary, coming into his office, is shocked to see him: My God, she says, you're back! I don't understand—did you see what they wrote about you?

The engineer sees fear in his secretary's eyes. What

can he do? He rushes to the *Rude Pravo* office. He finds the editor responsible for the story. The editor apologizes; yes, it really is an awkward business, but he, the editor, has nothing to do with it, he got the text of the article direct from the Ministry of the Interior.

So the engineer goes off to the Ministry. There they say yes, of course, it's all a mistake, but they, the Ministry, have nothing to do with it, they got the report on the engineer from the intelligence people at the London embassy. The engineer asks for a retraction. No, he's told, they never retract, but nothing can happen to him, he has nothing to worry about.

But the engineer does worry. He soon realizes that all of a sudden he's being closely watched, that his telephone is tapped, and that he's being followed in the street. He sleeps poorly and has nightmares until, unable to bear the pressure any longer, he takes a lot of real risks to leave the country illegally. And so he actually becomes an émigré.

2.

The story I've just told is one that we would immediately call *Kafkan*. This term, drawn from an artist's work, determined solely by a novelist's images, stands as the only common denominator in situations (literary or real) that no other word allows us to grasp and to which neither political nor social nor psychological theory gives us any key.

But what is the *Kafkan*?

Let's try to describe some of its aspects:

One:

The engineer is confronted by a power that has the character of a *boundless labyrinth*. He can never get to the end of its interminable corridors and will never succeed in finding out who issued the fateful verdict. He is therefore in the same situation as Joseph K. before the Court, or the Land-Surveyor K. before the Castle. All three are in a world that is nothing but a single, huge labyrinthine institution they cannot escape and cannot understand.

Novelists before Kafka often exposed institutions as arenas where conflicts between different personal and public interests were played out. In Kafka the institution is a mechanism that obeys its own laws; no one knows now who programmed those laws or when; they have nothing to do with human concerns and are thus unintelligible.

Two:

In Chapter Five of *The Castle*, the village Mayor explains in detail to K. the long history of his file. Briefly: Years earlier, a proposal to engage a land-surveyor came down to the village from the Castle. The Mayor wrote a negative response (there was no need for any land-surveyor), but his reply went astray to the wrong office, and so after an intricate series of bureaucratic misunderstandings, stretching over many years, the job offer was inadvertently sent to K., at the very moment when all the offices involved were in the process of canceling the old obsolete proposal. After a long journey, K. thus arrived in the village by mistake. Still more: Given that for him there is no possible world other than the Castle and its village, his *entire* existence is a mistake.

In the Kafkan world, the file takes on the role of a Platonic idea. It represents true reality, whereas man's physical existence is only a shadow cast on the screen of illusion. Indeed, both the Land-Surveyor K. and the Prague engineer are but the shadows of their file cards; and they are even much less than that: they are the shadows of a *mistake* in the file, shadows without even the right to exist as shadows.

But if man's life is only a shadow and true reality lies elsewhere, in the inaccessible, in the inhuman or the suprahuman, then we suddenly enter the domain of theology. Indeed, Kafka's first commentators explained his novels as religious parables.

Such an interpretation seems to me wrong (because it sees allegory where Kafka grasped concrete situations of human life) but also revealing: wherever power deifies itself, it automatically produces its own theology; wherever it behaves like God, it awakens religious feelings toward itself; such a world can be described in theological terms.

Kafka did not write religious allegories, but the *Kafkan* (both in reality and in fiction) is inseparable from its theological (or rather: *pseudotheological*) dimension.

Three:

Raskolnikov cannot bear the weight of his guilt, and to find peace he consents to his punishment of his own free will. It's the well-known situation where *the offense seeks the punishment*.

In Kafka the logic is reversed. The person punished does not know the reason for the punishment. The absurdity of the punishment is so unbearable that to find peace the accused needs to find a justification for his penalty: the *punishment seeks the offense.*

The Prague engineer is punished by intensive police surveillance. This punishment demands the crime that was not committed, and the engineer accused of emigrating ends up emigrating in fact. *The punishment has finally found the offense.*

Not knowing what the charges against him are, K. decides, in Chapter Seven of *The Trial,* to examine his whole life, his entire past "down to the smallest details." The "autoculpabilization" machine goes into motion. *The accused seeks his offense.*

One day, Amalia receives an obscene letter from a Castle official. Outraged, she tears it up. The Castle doesn't even need to criticize Amalia's rash behavior. Fear (the same fear our engineer saw in his secretary's eyes) acts all by itself. With no order, no perceptible sign from the Castle, everyone avoids Amalia's family like the plague.

Amalia's father tries to defend his family. But there is a problem: Not only is the source of the verdict impossible to find, but the verdict itself does not exist! To appeal, to request a pardon, you have to be convicted first! The father begs the Castle to state his daughter's crime. So it's not enough to say that the punishment seeks the offense. In this pseudotheological world, *the punished beg for recognition of their guilt*!

It often happens in Prague nowadays that someone fallen into disgrace cannot find even the most menial job. In vain he asks for certification of the fact that he has committed an offense and that his employment is forbidden. The verdict is nowhere to be found. And since in Prague work is a duty laid down by law, he ends up being charged with parasitism; that means he is guilty of avoiding work. *The punishment finds the offense.*

Four:

The tale of the Prague engineer is in the nature of a funny story, a joke: it provokes laughter.

Two gentlemen, perfectly ordinary fellows (not "inspectors," as in the French translation), surprise Joseph K. in bed one morning, tell him he is under arrest, and eat up his breakfast. K. is a well-disciplined civil servant: instead of throwing the men out of his flat, he stands in his nightshirt and gives a lengthy self-defense. When Kafka read the first chapter of *The Trial* to his friends, everyone laughed, including the author.

Philip Roth's imagined film version of *The Castle:* Groucho Marx plays the Land-Surveyor K., with Chico and Harpo as the two assistants. Yes, Roth is quite right: The comic is inseparable from the very essence of the *Kafkan.*

But it's small comfort to the engineer to know that his story is comic. He is trapped in the joke of his own life like a fish in a bowl; he doesn't find it funny. Indeed, a joke is a joke only if you're outside the bowl; by contrast, the *Kafkan* takes us inside, into the guts of a joke, into the *horror of the comic.*

In the world of the *Kafkan,* the comic is not a counterpoint to the tragic (the tragicomic) as in Shakespeare; it's not there to make the tragic more bearable by lightening the tone; it doesn't *accompany* the tragic, not at all, it *nips it in the bud* and thus deprives the victims of the only consolation they could hope for: the consolation to be found in the (real or supposed) grandeur of tragedy. The engineer loses his homeland, and everyone laughs.

3.

There are periods of modern history when life resembles the novels of Kafka.

When I was still living in Prague, I would frequently hear people refer to the Party headquarters (an ugly, rather modern building) as "the Castle." Just as frequently, I would hear the Party's second-in-command (a certain Comrade Hendrych) called "Klamm" (which was all the more beautiful as *klam* in Czech means "mirage" or "fraud").

The poet N., a great Communist personage, was imprisoned after a Stalinist trial in the fifties. In his cell he wrote a collection of poems in which he declared himself faithful to Communism despite all the horrors he had experienced. That was not out of cowardice. The poet saw his faithfulness (faithfulness to his persecutors) as the mark of his virtue, of his rectitude. Those in Prague who came to know of this collection gave it, with fine irony, the title "The Gratitude of Joseph K."

The images, the situations, and even the individual sentences of Kafka's novels were part of life in Prague.

That said, one might be tempted to conclude: Kafka's images are alive in Prague because they anticipate totalitarian society.

This claim, however, needs to be corrected: the *Kafkan* is not a sociological or a political notion. Attempts have been made to explain Kafka's novels as a critique of industrial society, of exploitation, alienation, bourgeois morality—of capitalism, in a word. But there is almost nothing of the constituents of capitalism in Kafka's universe: not money or its power, not commerce, not property and owners or the class struggle.

Neither does the *Kafkan* correspond to a definition of totalitarianism. In Kafka's novels, there is neither the party nor ideology and its jargon nor politics, the police, or the army.

So we should rather say that the *Kafkan* represents one fundamental possibility of man and his world, a possibility that is not historically determined and that accompanies man more or less eternally.

But this correction does not dispose of the question: How is it possible that in Prague Kafka's novels merge with real life while in Paris the same novels are read as the hermetic expression of an author's entirely subjective world? Does this mean that the possibility of man and his world known as *Kafkan* becomes concrete personal destiny more readily in Prague than in Paris?

There are tendencies in modern history that produce the *Kafkan* in the broad social dimension: the progressive concentration of power, tending to deify itself; the bureaucratization of social activity that turns all institutions into *boundless labyrinths;* and the resulting depersonalization of the individual.

Totalitarian states, as extreme concentrations of these tendencies, have brought out the close relationship between Kafka's novels and real life. But if in the West people are unable to see this relationship, it is not only because the society we call democratic is less Kafkan than that of today's Prague. It is also, it seems to me, because over here, the sense of the real is inexorably being lost.

In fact, the society we call democratic is also familiar with the process that bureaucratizes and depersonalizes; the entire planet has become a theater of this process. Kafka's novels are an imaginary, oneiric hyperbole of it; a totalitarian state is a prosaic and material hyperbole of it.

But why was Kafka the first novelist to grasp these tendencies, which appeared on history's stage so clearly and brutally only after his death?

4.

Mystifications and legends aside, there is no significant trace anywhere of Franz Kafka's political interests; in that sense, he is different from all his Prague friends, from Max Brod, Franz Werfel, Egon Erwin Kisch, and from all the avant-gardes that, claiming to know the direction of history, indulged in conjuring up the face of the future.

So how is it that not their works but those of their

solitary, introverted companion, immersed in his own life and his art, are recognized today as a sociopolitical prophecy, and are for that very reason banned in a large part of the world?

I pondered this mystery one day after witnessing a little scene in the home of an old friend of mine. The woman in question had been arrested in 1951 during the Stalinist trials in Prague, and convicted of crimes she hadn't committed. Hundreds of Communists were in the same situation at the time. All their lives they had entirely identified themselves with their Party. When it suddenly became their prosecutor, they agreed, like Joseph K., "to examine their whole lives, their entire past, down to the smallest details" to find the hidden offense and, in the end, to confess to imaginary crimes. My friend managed to save her own life because she had the extraordinary courage to refuse to undertake—as her comrades did, as the poet N. did—the "search for her offense." Refusing to assist her persecutors, she became unusable for the final show trial. So instead of being hanged she got away with life imprisonment. After fourteen years, she was completely rehabilitated and released.

This woman had a one-year-old child when she was arrested. On release from prison, she thus rejoined her fifteen-year-old son and had the joy of sharing her humble solitude with him from then on. That she became passionately attached to the boy is entirely comprehensible. One day I went to see them—by then her son was twenty-five. The mother, hurt and angry, was crying. The cause was utterly trivial: the son had overslept or something like that.

I asked the mother: "Why get so upset over such a trifle? Is it worth crying about? Aren't you over-doing it?"

It was the son who answered for his mother: "No, my mother's not overdoing it. My mother is a splen-did, brave woman. She resisted when everyone else cracked. She wants me to become a real man. It's true, all I did was oversleep, but what my mother reproached me for is something much deeper. It's my attitude. My selfish attitude. I want to become what my mother wants me to be. And with you as witness, I promise her I will."

What the Party never managed to do to the mother, the mother had managed to do to her son. She had forced him to identify with an absurd accusation, to "seek his offense," to make a public confession. I looked on, dumbfounded, at this Stalinist mini-trial, and I understood all at once that the psychological mechanisms that function in great (apparently incredible and inhuman) historical events are the same as those that regulate private (quite ordinary and very human) situations.

5.

The famous letter Kafka wrote and never sent to his father demonstrates that it was from the family, from the relationship between the child and the deified power of the parents, that Kafka drew his knowledge of the *technique of culpabilization*, which became a major theme of his fiction. In "The Judgment," a short story intimately bound up with the author's family experience, the father accuses the son and commands him to drown himself. The son accepts his fictitious guilt and throws himself into the river as docilely as, in a later work, his successor Joseph K., indicted by a mysterious organization, goes to be slaughtered. The similarity between the two accusations, the two culpabilizations, and the two executions reveals the link, in Kafka's work, between the family's private "totalitarianism" and that in his great social visions.

Totalitarian society, especially in its more extreme versions, tends to abolish the boundary between the public and the private; power, as it grows ever more opaque, requires the lives of citizens to be entirely transparent. The ideal of *life without secrets* corresponds to the ideal of the exemplary family: a citizen does not have the right to hide anything at all from the Party or the State, just as a child has no right to keep a secret from his father or his mother. In their propaganda, totalitarian societies project an idyllic smile: they want to be seen as "one big family."

It's often said that Kafka's novels express a passionate desire for community and human contact, that the rootless being who is K. has only one goal: to overcome the curse of solitude. Now, this is not only a cliché, a reductive interpretation, it is a misinterpretation.

The Land-Surveyor K. is not in the least pursuing people and their warmth, he is not trying to become "a man among men" like Sartre's Orestes; he wants acceptance not from a community but from an institution. To have it, he must pay dearly: he must renounce his solitude. And this is his hell: he is never alone, the two assistants sent by the Castle follow him always. When he first makes love with Frieda, the two men are there, sitting on the café counter over the lovers, and from then on they are never absent from their bed.

Not the curse of solitude but the *violation of solitude* is Kafka's obsession!

Karl Rossmann is constantly being harassed by everybody: his clothes are sold; his only photo of his parents is taken away; in the dormitory, beside his bed, boys box and now and again fall on top of him; two roughnecks named Robinson and Delamarche force him to move in with them and fat Brunelda, whose moans resound through his sleep.

Joseph K.'s story also begins with the rape of privacy: two unknown men come to arrest him in bed. From that day on, he never feels alone: the Court follows him, watches him, talks to him; his private life disappears bit by bit, swallowed up by the mysterious organization on his heels.

Lyrical souls who like to preach the abolition of secrets and the transparency of private life do not realize the nature of the process they are unleashing. The starting point of totalitarianism resembles the beginning of *The Trial*: you'll be taken unawares in your bed. They'll come just as your father and mother used to.

People often wonder whether Kafka's novels are projections of the author's most personal and private conflicts, or descriptions of an objective "social machine."

The *Kafkan* is not restricted to either the private or the public domain; it encompasses both. The public is the mirror of the private, the private reflects the public.

6.

In speaking of the microsocial practices that generate the *Kafkan*, I mean not only the family but also the organization in which Kafka spent all his adult life: the office.

Kafka's heroes are often seen as allegorical projections of the intellectual, but there's nothing intellectual about Gregor Samsa. When he wakes up metamorphosed into a beetle, he has only one concern: in this new state, how to get to the office on time. In his head he has nothing but the obedience and discipline to which his profession has accustomed him: he's an employee, a *functionary*, as are all Kafka's characters; a functionary not in the sense of a sociological type (as in Zola) but as one human possibility, as one of the elementary ways of being.

In the bureaucratic world of the functionary, first, there is no initiative, no invention, no freedom of action; there are only orders and rules: *it is the world of obedience*.

Second, the functionary performs a small part of a large administrative activity whose aim and horizons he cannot see: *it is the world where actions have become mechanical* and people do not know the meaning of what they do.

Third, the functionary deals only with unknown persons and with files: *it is the world of the abstract.*

To place a novel in this world of obedience, of the mechanical, and of the abstract, where the only human adventure is to move from one office to another, seems to run counter to the very essence of epic poetry. Thus the question: How has Kafka managed to transform such gray, antipoetical material into fascinating novels?

The answer can be found in a letter he wrote to Milena: "The office is not a stupid institution; it belongs more to the realm of the fantastic than of the stupid." The sentence contains one of Kafka's greatest secrets. He saw what no one else could see: not only the enormous importance of the bureaucratic phenomenon for man, for his condition and for his future, but also (even more surprisingly) the poetic potential contained in the phantasmic nature of offices.

But what does it mean to say the office belongs to the realm of the fantastic?

The Prague engineer would understand: a mistake in his file projected him to London; so he wandered around Prague, a veritable *phantom*, seeking his *lost body*, while the offices he visited seemed to him a *boundless labyrinth* from some unknown *mythology*.

The quality of the fantastic that he perceived in the bureaucratic world allowed Kafka to do what had seemed unimaginable before: he transformed the profoundly antipoetic material of a highly bureaucratized society into the great poetry of the novel; he transformed a very ordinary story of a man who cannot obtain a promised job (which is actually the story of *The Castle*) into myth, into epic, into a kind of beauty never before seen.

By expanding a bureaucratic setting to the gigantic dimensions of a universe, Kafka unwittingly succeeded in creating an image that fascinates us by its resemblance to a society he never knew, that of today's Prague.

A totalitarian state is in fact a single, immense administration: since all work in it is for the state, everyone of every occupation has become an *employee*. A worker is no longer a worker, a judge no longer a judge, a shopkeeper no longer a shopkeeper, a priest no longer a priest; they are all functionaries of the State. "I belong to the Court," the priest says to Joseph K. in the Cathedral. In Kafka, the lawyers, too, work for the Court. A citizen in today's Prague does not find that surprising. He would get no better legal defense than K. did. His lawyers don't work for the defendants either, but for the Court.

7.

In a cycle of one hundred quatrains that sound the gravest and most complex depths with an almost childlike simplicity, the great Czech poet writes:

Poets don't invent poems
The poem is somewhere behind
It's been there for a long long time
The poet merely discovers it.

For the poet, then, writing means breaking through a wall behind which something immutable ("the poem") lies hidden in darkness. That's why (because of this surprising and sudden unveiling) "the poem" striks us first as a *dazzlement*.

I read *The Castle* for the first time when I was fourteen, and the book will never enchant me so thoroughly again, even though all the vast understanding it contains (all the real import of the *Kafkan*) was incomprehensible to me then: I was dazzled.

Later on my eyes adjusted to the light of "the poem" and I began to see my own lived experience in what had dazzled me; yet the light was still there.

"The poem," says Jan Skacel, has been waiting for us, immutable, "for a long long time." However, in a world of perpetual change, is the immutable not a mere illusion?

No. Every situation is of man's making and can only contain what man contains; thus one can imagine that the situation (and all its metaphysical implications) has existed as a human possibility "for a long long time."

But in that case, what does history (the mutable) represent for the poet?

In the eyes of the poet, strange as it may seem, history is in a position similar to the poet's own: History does not *invent*, it *discovers*. Through new situations, history reveals what man is, what has been in him "for a long long time," what his possibilities are.

If "the poem" is already there, then it would be illogical to impute to the poet the gift of *foresight*; no, he "only discovers" a human possibility ("the poem" that has been there "a long long time") that History will in its turn discover one day.

Kafka made no prophecies. All he did was see what was "behind." He did not know that his seeing was also a fore-seeing. He did not intend to unmask a social system. He shed light on the mechanisms he knew from private and microsocial human practice, not suspecting that later developments would put those mechanisms into action on the great stage of history.

The hypnotic eye of power, the desperate search for one's own offense, exclusion and the anguish of being excluded, the condemnation to conformism, the phantasmic nature of reality and the magical reality of the file, the perpetual rape of private life, etc.—all these experiments that History has performed on man in its immense test tubes, Kafka performed (some years earlier) in his novels.

The convergence of the real world of totalitarian states with Kafka's "poem" will always be somewhat uncanny, and it will always bear witness that the poet's act, in its very essence, is incalculable; and paradoxical: the enormous social, political, and "prophetic" import of Kafka's novels lies precisely in their "nonengagement," that is to say, in their total autonomy from all political programs, ideological concepts, and futurological prognoses.

Indeed, if instead of seeking "the poem" hidden "somewhere behind" the poet "engages" himself to the service of a truth known from the outset (which comes forward on its own and is "out in front"), he has renounced the mission of poetry. And it matters little whether the preconceived truth is called revolution or dissidence, Christian faith or atheism, whether it is more justified or less justified; a poet who serves any truth other than the truth *to be discovered* (which is *dazzlement*) is a false poet.

If I hold so ardently to the legacy of Kafka, if I defend it as my personal heritage, it is not because I think it worthwhile to imitate the inimitable (and rediscover the *Kafkan*) but because it is such a tremendous example of the *radical autonomy* of the novel (of the poetry that is the novel). This autonomy allowed Franz Kafka to say things about our human condition (as it reveals itself in our century) that no social or political thought could ever tell us.

PART SIX

Sixty-three Words

In 1968 and 1969, The Joke *was translated into all the Western languages. But what surprises! In France, the translator rewrote the novel by ornamenting my style. In England, the publisher cut out all the reflective passages, eliminated the musicological chapters, changed the order of the parts, recomposed the novel. Another country: I meet my translator, a man who knows not a word of Czech. "Then how did you translate it?" "With my heart." And he pulls a photo of me from his wallet. He was so congenial that I almost believed it was actually possible to translate by some telepathy of the heart. Of course, it turned out to be much simpler: he had worked from the French rewrite, as had the translator in Argentina. Another country: the translation was done from the Czech. I open the book and happen on Helena's monologue. The long sentences that in my original go on for a whole paragraph at a time are broken up into a multitude of short ones. . . . The shock of* The Joke's *translations scarred me forever. All the more because for me, since practically speaking I no longer have the Czech audience, translations are* everything. *I therefore decided, a few years ago, to put some order into the foreign editions of my books. This involved a certain amount of conflict and fatigue: reading, checking, correcting my novels, old and new, in the three or four foreign languages I can read, completely took over a whole period of my life. . . .*

The writer who determines to supervise the translations of his books finds himself chasing after hordes of words like a shepherd after a flock of wild sheep—a sorry figure to himself, a laughable one to others. I suspect that my friend

Pierre Nora, editor of the magazine Le Débat, *recognized the sadly comical quality of my shepherd existence. One day, with barely disguised compassion, he told me: "Look, forget this torture, and instead write something for my magazine. The translations have forced you to think about every one of your words. So write your own personal dictionary. A dictionary for your novels. Put down your key words, your problem words, the words you love. . . ."*

Well, here it is.

APHORISM. From the Greek word *aphorismos*, meaning "definition." Aphorism: poetic form of definition. (See: DEFINITION.)

BEAUTY (and KNOWLEDGE). Those who, in the spirit of Broch, declare knowledge to be the novel's sole morality are betrayed by the metallic aura of "knowledge," a word too much compromised by its links with the sciences. So we have to add: Whatever aspects of existence the novel discovers, it discovers as the beautiful. The earliest novelists discovered adventure. Thanks to them we find adventure itself beautiful and wish to have it. Kafka described man in a situation of tragic entrapment. Kafkologists used to debate at length whether their author granted us any hope. No, not hope. Something else. Even that life-denying situation is revealed by Kafka as a strange, dark beauty. Beauty, the last triumph possible for man who can no longer hope. Beauty in art: the suddenly kindled light of the never-before-said. This light that radiates from the great novels time can never dim, for human existence is perpetually being forgotten by man, and thus the novelists' discoveries, however old they may be, will never cease to astonish us.

BETRAYAL. "But what is betrayal? Betrayal means breaking ranks. Betrayal means breaking ranks and going off into the unknown. Sabina knew of nothing more magnificent than going off into the unknown" (*The Unbearable Lightness of Being*).

BORDER. "It takes so little, so infinitely little for someone to find himself on the other side of the border, where everything—love, convictions, faith, history—no longer has meaning. The whole mystery of human life resides in the fact that it is spent in the immediate proximity of, and even in direct contact with, that border, that it is separated from it not by kilometers but by barely a millimeter" (*The Book of Laughter and Forgetting*).

CENTRAL EUROPE. Seventeenth century: The enormous force of the baroque imposes a certain cultural unity on the region, which is multinational and thus polycentric, with its shifting and indefinable boundaries. The lingering shadow of baroque Catholicism persists there into the eighteenth century: no Voltaire, no Fielding. In the hierarchy of the arts, music stands

at the top. From Haydn on (and up through Schoenberg and Bartók) the center of gravity of European
music is there. Nineteenth century: A few great poets,
but no Flaubert; the Biedermeier spirit: the veil of
the idyllic draped over the real. In the twentieth century, revolt. The greatest minds (Freud, the novelists)
revalidate what for centuries was ill known and
unknown: rational and demystifying lucidity; a sense
of the real; the novel. Their revolt is the exact opposite
of French modernism's, which is antirationalist, anti-
realist, lyrical (this will cause a good many misunderstandings). The pleiad of great Central European
novelists: Kafka, Hasek, Musil, Broch, Gombrowicz:
their aversion to romanticism; their love for the pre-
Balzac novel and for the libertine spirit (Broch inter-
preting kitsch as a plot by monogamous puritanism
against the Enlightenment); their mistrust of history
and of the glorification of the future; their modernism, which has nothing to do with the avant-garde's
illusions.

The destruction of the Hapsburg empire, and then,
after 1945, Austria's cultural marginality and the
political nonexistence of the other countries, make
Central Europe a premonitory mirror showing the
possible fate of all of Europe. Central Europe: a labo-
ratory of twilight.

CENTRAL EUROPE (and EUROPE). In a press release,
Broch's publisher places him in a highly Central
European context: Hofmannsthal, Svevo. Broch pro-
tests: If he must be compared to someone, let it be

Gide and Joyce! Was he thereby denying his "Central Europeanness"? No, he was only saying that national, regional contexts are useless for apprehending the meaning and the value of a work.

COLLABORATOR. Historical situations, always new, unveil man's constant possibilities and allow us to name them. Thus, in the course of the war against Nazism, the word "collaboration" took on a new meaning: putting oneself voluntarily at the service of a vile power. What a fundamental notion! How did humanity do without it until 1944? Now that the word has been found, we realize more and more that man's activity is by nature a collaboration. All those who extol the mass media din, advertising's imbecilic smile, the neglect of the natural world, indiscretion raised to the status of a virtue—they deserve to be called *collaborators with the modern.*

COMIC. By providing us with the lovely illusion of human greatness, the tragic brings us consolation. The comic is crueler: it brutally reveals the meaninglessness of everything. I suppose all things human have their comic aspect, which in certain cases is recognized, acknowledged, utilized, and in others is veiled. The real geniuses of the comic are not those who make us laugh hardest but those who reveal some *unknown realm of the comic.* History has always been considered an exclusively serious territory. But there is the undiscovered comic side to history. Just as there is the (hard-to-take) comic side to sexuality.

CZECHOSLOVAKIA. I never use the word in my novels, even though the action is generally set there. This composite word is too young (born in 1918), with no roots in time, no beauty, and it exposes the very nature of the thing it names: composite and too young (untested by time). It may be possible in a pinch to found a state on so frail a word, but not a novel. That is why, to designate my characters' country, I always use the old word "Bohemia." From the standpoint of political geography, it is incorrect (my translators often bridle), but from the standpoint of poetry, it is the only possible name.

DEFINITION. The novel's meditative texture is supported by the armature of a few abstract terms. If I hope to avoid falling into the slough where everyone thinks he understands everything without understanding anything, not only must I select those terms with utter precision, but I must define and redefine them. (See: BETRAYAL, BORDER, FATE, LIGHTNESS, LYRICISM.) A novel is often, it seems to me, nothing but a long quest for some elusive definitions.

DESTINY. There comes a moment when the image of our life parts company with the life itself, stands free, and, little by little, begins to rule us. Already in *The*

Joke: "I came to realize that there was no power capable of changing the image of my person lodged somewhere in the supreme court of human destinies; that this image (even though it bore no resemblance to me) was much more real than my actual self; that I was its shadow and not it mine; that I had no right to accuse it of bearing no resemblance to me, but rather that it was I who was guilty of the nonresemblance; and that the nonresemblance was my cross, which I could not unload on anyone else, which was mine alone to bear."

And in *The Book of Laughter and Forgetting:* "Destiny has no intention of lifting a finger for Mirek (for his happiness, his security, his good spirits, his health), whereas Mirek is ready to do everything for his destiny (for its grandeur, its clarity, its beauty, its style, its intelligible meaning). He felt responsible for his destiny, but his destiny did not feel responsible for him."

Conversely to Mirek, the hedonistic man in his forties in *Life Is Elsewhere* clings to "the idyll of his nondestiny." (See: IDYLL.) Indeed, a hedonist resists the transformation of his life into a destiny. Destiny vampirizes us, it weighs us down, it is like a ball and chain locked to our ankles. (The man in his forties, be it said in passing, is of all my characters the one closest to me.)

ELITISM. The word "elitism" only appeared in France in 1967, the word "elitist" not until 1968. For the first time in history, the very language threw a glare of negativity, even of mistrust, on the notion of elite.

Official propaganda in the Communist countries began to pummel elitism and elitists at that same time. It used the terms to designate not captains of industry or famous athletes or politicians but only the cultural elite: philosophers, writers, professors, historians, figures in film and the theater.

An amazing synchronism. It seems that in the whole of Europe the cultural elite is yielding to other elites. Over there, to the elite of the police apparatus. Here, to the elite of the mass media apparatus. No one will ever accuse these new elites of elitism. Thus the word "elitism" will soon be forgotten. (See: EUROPE.)

EUROPE. In the Middle Ages, European unity rested on the common religion. In the Modern Era, religion yielded its position to culture (to cultural creation), which came to embody the supreme values by which Europeans recognized themselves, defined and identified themselves. Now, in our own time, culture is in turn yielding its position. But to what and to whom? What sphere will provide the sort of supreme values that could unify Europe? Technology? The marketplace? Politics involving the democratic ideal, the principle of tolerance? But if that tolerance no longer has any rich creativity or any powerful thought to protect, will it not become empty and useless? Or can we take culture's abdication as a kind of deliverance, to be welcomed euphorically? I don't know. I merely believe I know that culture has already yielded. And thus the image of European unity slips away into the past. European: one who is nostalgic for Europe.

EXCITATION.   Not pleasure or climax or emotion or passion. Excitation is the basis of eroticism, its deepest enigma, its key term.

FLOW.   In one of his letters, Chopin describes his stay in England. He plays in the salons, and the ladies always use the same term to express their delight: "Ah, how beautiful! It flows like water!" Chopin found it exasperating, as I do when I hear a translation praised in the same terms: "It really flows." Partisans of "flowing" translation often object to my translators: "That's not the way to say it in German (in English, in Spanish, etc.)!" I reply: "It's not the way to say it in Czech either!" My dear Italian publisher, Roberto Calasso, declares: "The mark of a good translation is not its fluency but rather all those unusual and original formulations ["not the way to say it"] that the translator has been bold enough to preserve and defend." Including unaccustomed punctuation. I once left a publisher for the sole reason that he tried to change my semicolons to periods.

FORGETTING.   "The struggle of man against power is the struggle of memory against forgetting." That remark by Mirek, a character in *The Book of Laughter and Forgetting*, is often cited as the book's message.

This is because the first thing a reader recognizes in a novel is the "already known." The "already known" in that novel is Orwell's famous theme: the forgetting that a totalitarian regime imposes. But to me the originality of Mirek's story lay somewhere else entirely. This Mirek who is struggling with all his might to make sure he is not forgotten (he and his friends and their political battle) is at the same time doing his utmost to make people forget another person (his ex-mistress, whom he's ashamed of). Before it becomes a political issue, the will to forget is an existential one: man has always harbored the desire to rewrite his own biography, to change the past, to wipe out tracks, both his own and others'. The will to forget is very different from a simple temptation to deceive. Sabina has no reason to hide anything at all, yet she feels driven by the irrational urge to make people forget about her. Forgetting: absolute injustice and absolute solace at the same time.

GRAPHOMANIA. "Not a mania to write letters, personal diaries, or family chronicles (to write for oneself or one's close relations) but a mania to write books (to have a public of unknown readers)" (*The Book of Laughter and Forgetting*). The mania not to create a form but to impose one's self on others. The most grotesque version of the will to power.

HAT. Magical object. I remember a dream: A ten-year-old boy is standing at the edge of a pond, wearing a big black hat on his head. He throws himself into the water. They pull him out, drowned. He still has the black hat on his head.

IDEAS. My disgust for those who reduce a work to its ideas. My revulsion at being dragged into what they call "discussions of ideas." My despair at this era befogged with ideas and indifferent to works.

IDYLL. A word rarely used in France, but a concept important to Hegel, Goethe, Schiller: the condition of the world before the first conflict; or beyond conflicts; or with conflicts that are only misunderstandings, thus false conflicts. "Even though he enjoyed a colorful erotic life, the man in his forties was basically an idyllist . . ." (*Life Is Elsewhere*). The desire to reconcile erotic adventure and idyll is the very essence of hedonism—and the reason why man cannot attain the hedonist ideal.

IMAGINATION. "What did you mean by the story about Tamina on the children's island?" people ask me. That tale began as a dream that fascinated me; I dreamed it later in a half-waking state, and I broadened and deepened it as I wrote it. Its meaning? If you like: an oneiric image of an infantocratic future. (See: INFANTOCRACY.) However, the meaning did not precede the dream; the dream preceded the meaning. So the way to read the tale is to let the imagination carry one along. Not, above all, as a rebus to be decoded. By insisting on decoding him, the Kafkologists killed Kafka.

INEXPERIENCE.   The original title considered for *The Unbearable Lightness of Being:* "The Planet of Inexperience." Inexperience as a quality of the human condition. We are born one time only, we can never start a new life equipped with the experience we've gained from a previous one. We leave childhood without knowing what youth is, we marry without knowing what it is to be married, and even when we enter old age, we don't know what it is we're heading for: the old are innocent children of their old age. In that sense, man's world is the planet of inexperience.

INFANTOCRACY.   "A motorcyclist rode down the empty street, arms and legs rounded in an O, and came back up with the sound of thunder; his face displayed the seriousness of a child who attributes the utmost importance to his howls" (Musil, in *The Man Without Qualities*). The seriousness of a child: the face of the technological era. Infantocracy: the ideal of childhood imposed on all of humanity.

INTERVIEW.   Cursed be the writer who first allowed a journalist to reproduce his remarks freely! He started the process that can only lead to the disappearance of the writer: he who is responsible for every one of his words. Yet I do very much like the *dialogue* (a major literary form), and I've been pleased with several such discussions that were mutually pondered, composed, and edited. Alas, the interview as it is generally practiced has nothing to do with a dialogue: (1) the interviewer asks questions of interest to him, of no interest to you; (2) of your responses, he uses only those that suit him; (3) he translates them into his own vocabulary, his own manner of thought. In imitation of American journalism, he will not even deign to get your approval for what he has you say. The interview appears. You console yourself: people will quickly forget it! Not at all: people will quote it! Even the most scrupulous academics no longer distinguish between the words a writer has written and signed, and his remarks as reported. (Historical precedent: Gustav Janouch's *Conversations with Kafka*, a hoax that is a bottomless source of quotes for Kafkologists.) In July 1985, I made a firm decision: no more interviews. Except for dialogues co-edited by me, *accompanied by my copyright,* all my reported remarks since then are to be considered forgeries.

IRONY.   Which is right and which is wrong? Is Emma Bovary intolerable? Or brave and touching? And what about Werther? Is he sensitive and noble? Or an aggressive sentimentalist, infatuated with himself? The more attentively we read a novel, the more impossible the answer, because the novel is, by definition, the ironic art: its "truth" is concealed, undeclared, undeclarable. "Remember, Razumov, that women, children, and revolutionists hate irony, which is the negation of all saving instincts, of all faith, of all devotion, of all action," says a Russian woman revolutionary in Joseph Conrad's *Under Western Eyes*. Irony irritates. Not because it mocks or attacks but because it denies us our certainties by unmasking the world as an ambiguity. Leonardo Sciascia: "There is nothing harder to understand, more indecipherable than irony." It is futile to try and make a novel "difficult" through stylistic affectation; any novel worth the name, however limpid it may be, is difficult enough by reason of its consubstantial irony.

KITSCH. In the course of writing *The Unbearable Lightness of Being*, I was a little uncomfortable at having made the word "kitsch" one of the key terms of the novel. Indeed, even recently, the term was nearly unknown in France, or known only in a very impoverished sense. In the French version of Hermann Broch's celebrated essay, the word "kitsch" is translated as "junk art" (*art de pacotille*). A misinterpretation, for Broch demonstrates that kitsch is something other than simply a work in poor taste. There is a kitsch attitude. Kitsch behavior. The kitsch-person's (*Kitschmensch*) need for kitsch: it is the need to gaze into the mirror of the beautifying lie and to be moved to tears of gratification at one's own reflection. For Broch, kitsch is historically bound to the sentimental romanticism of the nineteenth century. Because in Germany and Central Europe the nineteenth century was far more romantic (and far less realistic) than elsewhere, it was there that kitsch flowered to excess, it is there that the word "kitsch" was born, there that it is still in common use. In Prague, we saw kitsch as art's prime enemy. Not in France. For the French, the opposite of real art is entertainment. The opposite of serious art is light, minor art. But for my part, I never minded Agatha Christie's detective novels. Whereas Tchaikovsky, Rachmaninoff, Horowitz at the piano, the big Hollywood films like *Kramer vs. Kramer*, *Doctor Zhivago* (poor Pasternak!)—those I detest, deeply, sincerely. And I am more and more irritated by the kitsch spirit in certain works whose form pretends to modernism. (I add: Nietzsche's hatred for Victor Hugo's "pretty words" and "ceremonial dress" was a disgust for kitsch *avant la lettre*.)

LAUGHTER (European). For Rabelais, the merry and the comic were still one and the same. In the eighteenth century, the humor of Sterne and Diderot is an affectionate, nostalgic recollection of Rabelaisian merriment. In the nineteenth century, Gogol is a melancholy humorist: "The longer and more carefully we look at a funny story, the sadder it becomes," said he. Europe has looked for such a long time at the funny story of its own existence that in the twentieth century, Rabelais's merry epic has turned into the despairing comedy of Ionesco, who says, "There's only a thin line between the horrible and the comic." The European history of laughter comes to an end.

LETTERS. They are getting smaller and smaller in books these days. I imagine the death of literature: Bit by bit, without anyone noticing, the type shrinks until it becomes utterly invisible.

LIFE (with a capital L).   In the surrealists' pamphlet *A Cadaver* (1924), Paul Éluard sharply addresses Anatole France's corpse: "We do not love those who resemble you, o cadaver . . . ," etc. More interesting than this kick at a coffin, I think, is the justification that follows: "What I can no longer imagine without tears in my eyes, Life, still turns up today in derisory little things now sustained by tenderness alone. Skepticism, irony, cowardice, France, the French mind— what are these? A great gust of forgetting sweeps me far away from all that. Have I perhaps never read anything, seen anything, that dishonors Life?"

Éluard was opposed to skepticism and irony: the derisory little things, the tears in the eyes, the tenderness, the honor of life, yes, Life with a capital L! Behind the spectacularly nonconformist gesture, the spirit of kitsch at its dullest.

LIGHTNESS.   I see that the unbearable lightness of being was already in evidence in *The Joke:* "I strode across those dusty cobblestones under the oppressive lightness of the void lying over my life."

And in *Life Is Elsewhere:* "Jaromil sometimes had terrible dreams: he dreamed that he had to lift some extremely light object—a teacup, a spoon, a feather— and he couldn't do it, that the lighter the object, the weaker he became, that he *sank under its lightness.*"

And in *Farewell Waltz:* "Raskolnikov experienced his crime as a tragedy, and eventually he was overwhelmed by the weight of his act. Jakub was amazed that his act was so light, so weightless, amazed that it did not overwhelm him. And he wondered if this lightness was not more terrifying than the Russian character's hysterical feelings."

In *The Book of Laughter and Forgetting:* "That hollowness in her stomach is exactly that unbearable absence of weight. And just as an extreme can at any moment turn into its opposite, so lightness brought to its maximum becomes the terrifying *weight of lightness,* and Tamina knows she cannot bear it for another moment."

Only when I reread my books in translation did I see, with consternation, all those recurrences! Then I consoled myself; perhaps all novelists ever do is write a kind of *theme* (the first novel) *and variations.*

LITANY. Repetition: a principle of music composition. Litany: speech become music. I should like to see the novel, in its reflective passages, turn into song from time to time. Here is a litany passage from *The Joke,* composed around the word "home":

". . . and it seemed to me that inside these songs I was *at home*, that I derive from them, and if I had betrayed this home, I had only made it *all the more* my home (because what voice is more plaintive than the voice of the home we have betrayed?); but I was equally aware that this home was not of this world (though what kind of home was it if it wasn't of this world?), that what we were singing and playing were only memories, recollections, an imaginary preservation of something that no longer was, and I felt the ground of this home sinking under my feet, felt myself falling, clarinet in mouth, falling down into the depths of years, the depths of centuries, into the fathomless depths, and I told myself with astonishment that my only home was this descent, this searching, eager fall, and I abandoned myself to it and to my sweet vertigo." (See REPETITIONS.)

LYRICAL.   In *The Unbearable Lightness of Being*, there is a discussion of two types of womanizer: the lyrical (who seek their personal ideal in each woman) and the epical (who seek in women the infinite variety of the feminine universe). This corresponds to the classical distinction between the lyrical and the epical (and the dramatic), a distinction that appeared only toward the end of the eighteenth century in Germany and that was masterfully developed in Hegel's *Aesthetics:* The lyrical is the expression of a self-revealing subjectivity; the epical arises from the urge to seize hold of the objectivity of the world. For me, the lyrical and the epical extend beyond aesthetics; they represent two possible attitudes that man might take toward himself, the world, other people (the lyrical age = youth). Alas, such a conception of lyrical and epical is so unfamiliar to the French that I was obliged to let the translator turn the lyrical womanizer into the romantic fornicator, and the epical womanizer into the libertine fornicator. The best solution—but still it made me a little sad.

LYRICISM (and revolution).   "Lyricism is intoxication, and man drinks in order to merge more easily with the world. Revolution has no desire to be examined or analyzed, it only desires that the people merge with it; in this sense it is lyrical and in need of lyricism" (*Life Is Elsewhere*). "The wall behind which people were imprisoned was made entirely of verse, and in front of the wall there was dancing. No, not a *danse macabre*. Here innocence danced! Innocence with its bloody smile" (*Life Is Elsewhere*).

MACHO (and MISOGYNIST).   The macho adores femaleness and wants to dominate what he adores. By glorifying the archetypal femaleness of the dominated woman (her motherhood, her fertility, her frailty, her home-loving nature, her sentimentality, etc.), he glorifies his own virility. The misogynist, on the other hand, is repelled by femaleness; he flees women who are too womanly. The macho's ideal: the family. The misogynist's ideal: the bachelor with a great many mistresses; or: marriage to a beloved childless woman.

MEDITATION.   Three elementary possibilities for the novelist: he *tells* a story (Fielding), he *describes* a story (Flaubert), he *thinks* a story (Musil). The nineteenth-century novel of description was in harmony with the (positivist, scientific) spirit of the time. To base a novel on a sustained meditation goes against the spirit of the twentieth century, which no longer likes to think at all.

METAPHOR.   I do not like it when it is merely ornament. And I am thinking not only of clichés like "the green carpet of a meadow," but also, for instance, of Rilke's "Their laughter oozed from their mouths as from running sores." Or: "Already his prayer drops its leaves and juts out of his mouth like a dead shrub." (*The Notebooks of Malte Laurids Brigge*). On the other hand, metaphor seems to me indispensable as a means of grasping, through instantaneous revelation, the ungraspable essence of things, situations, characters. The metaphor-definition. For instance in Broch, Esch's existential attitude: "He wanted unambiguous clarity: he wanted to create a world of such clear simplicity that his solitude might be bound to that clarity as to an iron post." (*The Sleepwalkers.*) My rule: very few metaphors in a novel; but those there are must be its peaks.

MISOGYNIST.   From our earliest days every one of us is faced with a mother and a father, a femininity and a masculinity. And thus marked by a harmonious or disharmonious relation with each of these two archetypes. Gynophobes (misogynists) occur not only among men but among women as well, and there are as many gynophobes as there are androphobes (men and women who live in disharmony with the masculine archetype). Both these attitudes are fully legitimate possibilities of the human condition. Feminist manicheism has never considered the issue of androphobia and has transformed misogyny into mere insult. Thus the psychological component of the notion, the only one that is interesting, is evaded.

MISOMUSIST. To be without a feeling for art is no disaster. A person can live in peace without reading Proust or listening to Schubert. But the misomusist does not live in peace. He feels humiliated by the existence of something that is beyond him, and he hates it. There is a popular misomusy just as there is a popular anti-Semitism. The fascist and Communist regimes made use of it when they declared war on modern art. But there is an intellectual, sophisticated misomusy as well: it takes revenge on art by forcing it to a purpose beyond the aesthetic. The doctrine of *engagé* art: art as an instrument of politics. The theoreticians for whom a work of art is merely the pretext for deploying a method (psychoanalytic, semiological, sociological, etc.). Democratic misomusy: the market as supreme arbiter of aesthetic value.

MODERN (modern art; modern world). There is the modern art that, in *lyrical* ecstasy, identifies with the modern world. Apollinaire. Glorification of the technical, fascination with the future. Along with and after him: Mayakovsky, Léger, the Futurists, the various avant-gardes. But opposite Apollinaire is Kafka: the modern world seen as a labyrinth where man loses his way. The modernism that is *antilyrical*, antiromantic, skeptical, critical. With Kafka and after him: Musil, Broch, Gombrowicz, Beckett, Ionesco, Fellini. . . . The farther we advance into the future, the greater becomes this legacy of "antimodern modernism."

MODERN (being modern). "New, new, new is the star of Communism, and there is no modernity outside it," wrote the great Czech avant-garde novelist Vladislav Vancura around 1920. His whole generation rushed to the Communist Party so as not to miss out on being modern. The historical decline of the Communist Party was sealed once it fell everywhere "outside modernity." Because, as Rimbaud commanded, "it is necessary to be absolutely modern." The desire to be modern is an archetype, that is, an irrational imperative, anchored deeply within us, a persistent form whose content is changeable and indeterminate: what is modern is what declares itself modern and is accepted as such. Mrs. Youthful in Gombrowicz's *Ferdydurke* displays as one of the marks of modernity "her casual way of heading for the toilet, where till then people had gone in secret." *Ferdydurke:* the most dazzling demythification of the archetype of the modern.

MYSTIFICATION. Neologism, amusing in itself (derived from the word "mystery"), appearing in

France in the eighteenth century within the world of libertine wit to describe practical jokes whose entire purpose is comical. Diderot was forty-seven when he set up a remarkable hoax that got the Marquis de Croismare to believe that an unhappy young nun was asking to put herself under his protection. Over the course of several months Diderot sent the excited marquis letters signed by a nonexistent woman. His novel *The Nun* was born of that hoax: one more reason to love Diderot and his century. Mystification: the active form of refusing to take the world seriously.

NONBEING. "... death sweetly bluish like nonbeing" (*The Book of Laughter and Forgetting*). We cannot say "bluish like nothingness," because nothingness is not bluish. Proof that nothingness and nonbeing are two entirely different things.

NOVEL. The great prose form in which an author thoroughly explores, by means of experimental selves (characters), some themes of existence.

NOVEL (and poetry). 1857: the greatest year of the century. *Les Fleurs du mal*: lyrical poetry discovers its rightful territory, its essence. *Madame Bovary*: for the first time, a novel is ready to take on the highest requirements of poetry (the determination to "seek beauty above all"; the importance of each particular word; the intense melody of the text; the imperative of originality applied to every detail). From 1857 on, the history of the novel will be that of the "novel become poetry." But *to take on the requirements of poetry* is quite another thing from *lyricizing* the novel (forgoing its essential irony, turning away from the outside world, transforming the novel into personal confession, weighing it down with ornament). The greatest of the "novelists become poets" are violently *antilyrical*: Flaubert, Joyce, Kafka, Gombrowicz. Novel: antilyrical poetry.

NOVEL (European).   The novel I term European takes form in Southern Europe at the dawn of the Modern Era and in itself represents a historic entity that will go on to expand its territory beyond geographic Europe (most notably into both Americas). In the richness of its forms, the dizzyingly concentrated intensity of its evolution, and its social role, the European novel (like European music) has no equal in any other civilization.

NOVELIST (and writer).   I reread Sartre's short essay "What Is Writing?" Not once does he use the words "novel" or "novelist." He only speaks of the "prose writer." A proper distinction. The writer has original ideas and an inimitable voice. He may use any form (including the novel), and whatever he writes—being marked by his thought, borne by his voice—is part of his work. Rousseau, Goethe, Chateaubriand, Gide, Malraux, Camus.

The novelist makes no great issue of his ideas. He is an explorer feeling his way in an effort to reveal some unknown aspect of existence. He is fascinated not by his voice but by a form he is seeking, and only those forms that meet the demands of his dream become part of his work. Fielding, Sterne, Flaubert, Proust, Faulkner, Céline.

The writer inscribes himself on the spiritual map of his time, of his country, on the map of the history of ideas.

The only context for grasping a novel's worth is the history of the European novel. The novelist need answer to no one but Cervantes.

NOVELIST (and his life).   "The artist must make posterity believe he never lived," Flaubert said. Maupassant kept his portrait from appearing in a series on famous writers: "A man's private life and his face do not belong to the public." Hermann Broch said about himself, Musil, Kafka: "The three of us have no real biographies." Which does not mean that their lives were meager in event, but that they were not destined to be noteworthy, to be public, to become bio-graphy. Someone asks Karel Capek why he doesn't write poetry. His answer: "Because I loathe talking about myself." The distinctive feature of the true novelist: he does not like to talk about himself. "I hate tampering with the precious lives of great writers, and no biographer will ever catch a glimpse of my private life," said Nabokov. Italo Calvino warned: no one should expect a single true word from him about his own life. And Faulkner wished "to be, as a private individual, abolished and voided from history, leaving it markless, no refuse save the printed books." (Underline: *books* and *printed*, meaning no unfinished manuscripts, no letters, no diaries.) According to a well-known metaphor, the novelist demolishes the house of his life and uses its bricks to construct another house: that of his novel. From which it follows that a novelist's biographers unmake what the novelist made, and remake what he unmade. Their labor, from the standpoint of art utterly negative, can illuminate neither the value nor the meaning of a novel. The moment Kafka draws more attention than Joseph K., the process of Kafka's posthumous dying begins.

OBSCENITY.   We can use obscene words in a foreign language, but they are not heard as such. An obscenity pronounced with an accent becomes comical. The difficulty of being obscene with a foreign woman. Obscenity: the root that attaches us most deeply to our homeland.

OCTAVIO.   I am in the midst of construction this little dictionary when the terrible earthquake rocks Mexico City, where Octavio Paz lives with his wife, Marie-Jo. Nine days with no word of them. On September 27, a phone call: a message from Octavio. I open a bottle to toast him. And I make his dear, dear name the forty-ninth of these sixty-three words.

OLD AGE.   "The old scholar was watching the noisy young people around him, and it suddenly occurred to him that he was the only one in the whole audience who had the privilege of freedom, for he was old; when he is old a man is no longer obliged to care about his group's opinions, about the public, and about the future. He is alone with approaching death, and death has neither eyes nor ears, he has no need to please death; he can do and say what he pleases" (*Life Is Elsewhere*). Rembrandt and Picasso. Bruckner and Janacek. The Bach of *The Art of the Fugue*.

OPUS.   The excellent custom of composers. They give opus numbers only to works they see as "valid." They do not number works written in their immature period, or occasional pieces, or technical exercises. An unnumbered Beethoven composition—for instance, the "Salieri" Variations—though it may be quite weak, does not disappoint us, for the composer himself has alerted us. A fundamental question for any artist: Which is his first "valid" work? Janacek found his own voice only after he was forty-five; I suffer when I hear the few compositions still extant from his previous period. Just before he died, Debussy destroyed all his sketches, everything he had left unfinished. The least an author can do for his works: sweep up around them.

PSEUDONYM. I dream of a world where writers will be required by law to keep their identities secret and to use pseudonyms. Three advantages: a drastic reduction of graphomania; decreased aggressiveness in literary life; the disappearance of biographical interpretation of works.

REFLECTION. The hardest to translate: not dialogue or description but reflective passages. Not only must their absolute accuracy be preserved (any semantic unfaithfulness renders the reflection false), but so must their beauty. The beauty of reflection shows in the *poetic forms of reflection*. I can name three: (1) aphorism, (2) litany, (3) metaphor. (See: APHORISM, LITANY, METAPHOR.)

REPETITIONS. Nabokov points out that at the beginning of the Russian text of *Anna Karenina* the word "house" occurs eight times in six sentences and that the repetition is a deliberate tactic on the author's part. Yet the word "house" appears only once in the French translation of the passage, and no more than twice in the Czech. In that same book: where Tolstoy repeatedly writes *skazal* ("said"), the French translation uses "remarked," "retorted," "responded," "cried," "stated," etc. Translators are crazy about synonyms. (I reject the very notion of synonym: each word has its own meaning and is semantically irreplaceable.) Pascal: "When words are repeated in a text and in trying to replace them we find them so apt that doing so would spoil the text, they should be left in, they are the benchmark of the piece." Richness of vocabulary is not a value in itself: in Hemingway, it is the limitation of vocabulary, the repetition of the same words in the same paragraph, that makes the melody and the beauty of the style. The playful elegance of repetition in the first paragraph of one of the loveliest pieces of French prose, the eighteenth-century novel *Point de lendemain* ("No Tomorrow") by Vivant Denon: *"J'aimais éperdument la Comtesse de . . . ; j'avais vingt ans, et j'étais ingénu; elle me trompa, je me fâchai, elle me quitta. J'étais ingénu, je la regrettai; j'avais vingt ans, elle me pardonna: et comme j'avais vingt ans, que j'étais ingénu, toujours trompé, mais plus quitté, je me croyais l'amant le mieux aimé, partant le plus heureux des hommes. . . ."* ("I was madly in love with the Comtesse de . . . ; I was twenty, and I was naive; she cuckolded me, I protested, she deserted me. I was naive, I longed for her; I was twenty, she forgave me; and because I was twenty, was naive, was still cuckolded but no longer deserted, I thought myself the best beloved of her lovers, and thus the happiest man alive.") (See: LITANY.)

REWRITING.   Interviews. Adaptations, transcriptions for the theater, for film, for television. Rewriting as the spirit of the times. "One day all past culture will be completely rewritten and completely forgotten behind the rewrite" (Introduction to *Jacques and His Master*). And: "Death to all who dare rewrite what has been written! Impale them and roast them over a slow fire! Castrate them and cut off their ears!" (The Master in *Jacques and His Master*).

RHYTHM. I hate to hear the beat of my heart; it is a relentless reminder that the minutes of my life are numbered. So I have always seen something macabre in the bar lines that measure out a musical score. But the greatest masters of rhythm know how to silence that monotonous and predictable regularity. The masters of polyphony: contrapuntal, horizontal thinking weakens the importance of the measure. In late Beethoven, the rhythm is so complicated, especially in the slow movements, that we can barely make out the bar lines. My admiration for Olivier Messiaen: with his technique of small rhythmic values added or subtracted, he invents an unforeseeable and incalculable time structure. A received idea: that the genius of rhythm is expressed through noisy, emphatic regularity. False. The tedious rhythmic primitivism of rock: the heart's beat is amplified so that man can never for a moment forget his march toward death.

SOVIET. An adjective I do not use. Union of Soviet Socialist Republics: "Four words, four lies" (Cornelius Castoriadis). The Soviet people: a verbal screen behind which all the Russified nations of that Empire are meant to be forgotten. The term "Soviet" is appropriate not only for the aggressive nationalism of Communist Greater Russia but also for the national pride of the Russian dissidents. It allows them to believe that through a feat of magic, Russia (the real Russia) has been removed from the so-called Soviet State and somehow survives as an intact, immaculate essence, free of all blame. The German conscience: traumatized, incriminated by the Nazi era; Thomas Mann: pitiless arraignment of the Germanic spirit. The ripest moment of Polish culture: Gombrowicz joyously excoriating "Polishness." Unthinkable for the Russians to excoriate "Russianness," that immaculate essence. Not a Mann, not a Gombrowicz among them.

Temps modernes (Modern Era).   The coming of *les Temps modernes*. The key moment of European history. In the seventeenth century, God becomes *Deus absconditus* and man the ground of all things. European individualism is born, and with it a new situation for art, for culture, for science. I run into problems with this term in the United States. The literal translation, "modern times" (and even the more comprehensive "Modern Era"), an American takes to mean the contemporary moment, our century. The absence in America of the notion of *les Temps modernes* reveals the great chasm between the two continents. In Europe, we are living the end of the Modern Era: the end of individualism; the end of art conceived as an irreplaceable expression of personal originality; the end that heralds an era of unparalleled uniformity. This sense of ending America does not feel, for America did not live through the birth of the Modern Era and has only come along lately to inherit it.

America has other criteria for beginnings and endings.

TESTAMENT.   Nowhere in the world nor in any form whatsoever may there occur the publication or reproduction of anything I ever wrote (or will write) except for the books of mine listed in the most recent Gallimard catalog. And no annotated editions. No adaptations. (See: OPUS, REWRITING, WORK.) [Entry added in the 1995 French printing.]

TRANSPARENCY.   A very common term in political and journalistic discourse in Europe. It means: the exposure of individual lives to public view. Which sends us back to André Breton and his wish to live in a *glass house* in full view. The glass house: an old utopian idea and at the same time one of the most horrifying aspects of modern life. Axiom: The more opaque the affairs of state, the more transparent an individual's affairs must be; though it represents a *public thing*, bureaucracy is anonymous, secret, coded, inscrutable, whereas *private man* is obliged to reveal his health, his finances, his family situation, and if the mass media so decree, he will never again have a single moment of privacy either in love or in sickness or in death. The urge to violate another's privacy is an age-old form of aggression that in our day is institutionalized (bureaucracy with its documents, the press with its reporters), justified morally (the right to know having become first among the rights of man), and poeticized (by the lovely French word *transparence*).

UNIFORM (uni-form). "Since reality consists in the uniformity of calculable reckoning, man, too, must enter monotonous uniformity in order to keep up with what is real. A man without a uni-form today already gives the impression of being something unreal which no longer belongs" (Heidegger, "Overcoming Metaphysics"). The Land-Surveyor K. is engaged not in a search for brotherhood but in a desperate search for a uni-form. Without that uni-form, without the uniform of an employee, he cannot "keep up with what is real," he "gives the impression of being something unreal." Kafka was the first (before Heidegger) to grasp this shift in situation: yesterday it was still possible to see in pluriformity, in an avoidance of the uniform, an ideal, a stroke of luck, a triumph; by tomorrow the loss of the uniform will represent a drastic misfortune, an exclusion from what is human. Since Kafka's time, because of the great systems that quantify and plan life, the uniformization of the world has made enormous advances. But when a phenomenon becomes universal, quotidian, omnipresent, we no longer notice it. In the euphoria of their uni-form lives, people no longer see the uniform they wear.

VALUE. The structuralism of the sixties made the question of value parenthetical. And yet the founder of structuralist aesthetics says: "Only the assumption of objective aesthetic value gives meaning to the historical evolution of art" (Jan Mukarovsky: *Aesthetic Function, Norm, and Value as Social Facts*, Prague, 1934). To examine an aesthetic value means: to try to demarcate and give name to the discoveries, the innovations, the new light that a work casts on the human world. Only the work acknowledged as value (the work whose newness has been apprehended and named) can become part of the "historical evolution of art," which is not a mere succession of events but an intentional pursuit of values. If we reject the question of value and settle for a description (thematic, sociological, formalist) of a work (of a historical period, culture, etc.); if we equate all cultures and all cultural activities (Bach and rock, comic strips and Proust); if the criticism of art (meditation on value) can no longer find room for expression, then the "historical evolution of art" will lose its meaning, will crumble, will turn into a vast and absurd storehouse of works.

WORK.   "From the sketch to the work one travels on one's knees." I cannot forget that line from Vladimir Holan. And I refuse to put the *Letters to Felice* on the same level as *The Castle*.

154

PART SEVEN

Jerusalem Address:
The Novel and Europe

That Israel's most important prize is awarded to international literature is not, to my mind, a matter of chance but of a long tradition. Indeed, exiled from their land of origin and thus lifted above nationalist passions, the great Jewish figures have always shown an exceptional feeling for a supranational Europe—a Europe conceived not as territory but as culture. If the Jews, even after Europe so tragically failed them, nonetheless kept faith with that European cosmopolitanism, Israel, their little homeland finally regained, strikes me as the true heart of Europe—a peculiar heart located outside the body.

It is with profound emotion that I receive today the prize that bears the name of Jerusalem and the mark of that great cosmopolitan Jewish spirit. It is as a novelist that I accept it. I say *novelist*, not writer. The novelist is one who, according to Flaubert, seeks to disappear behind his work. To disappear behind his work, that is, to renounce the role of public figure. This is not easy these days, when anything of the slightest importance must step into the intolerable glare of the mass media, which, contrary to Flaubert's precept, cause the work to disappear behind the image of its author. In such a situation, which no one can entirely escape, Flaubert's remark seems to me a kind of warning: in lending himself to the role of public figure, the novelist endangers his work; it risks being considered a mere appendage to his actions, to his declarations, to his statements of position. Now, not only is the novelist nobody's spokesman, but I would go so far as to say he is not even the spokesman for his own ideas. When Tolstoy sketched the first draft of *Anna Karenina*, Anna was a most unsympathetic woman, and her tragic end was entirely deserved and justified. The final version of the novel is very different, but I do not believe that Tolstoy had revised his moral ideas in the meantime; I would say, rather, that in the course of writing, he was listening to another voice than that of his personal moral conviction. He was listening to what I would like to call the wisdom of the novel. Every true novelist listens for that suprapersonal wisdom, which explains why great novels are always a little more intelligent than their authors. Novelists who are more intelligent than their books should go into another line of work.

But what is that wisdom, what is the novel? There is a fine Jewish proverb: Man thinks, God laughs. Inspired by that adage, I like to imagine that François Rabelais heard God's laughter one day, and thus was born the idea of the first great European novel. It pleases me to think that the art of the novel came into the world as the echo of God's laughter.

But why does God laugh at the sight of man thinking? Because man thinks and the truth escapes him. Because the more men think, the more one man's thought diverges from another's. And finally, because man is never what he thinks he is. The dawn of the Modern Era revealed this fundamental situation of man as he emerged from the Middle Ages: Don Quixote thinks, Sancho thinks, and not only the world's truth but also the truth of their own selves slips away from them. The first European novelists saw, and grasped, that new situation of man, and on it they built the new art, the art of the novel.

François Rabelais invented a number of neologisms that have since entered the French and other languages, but one of his words has been forgotten, and this is regrettable. It is the word *agélaste*; it comes from the Greek and it means a man who does not laugh, who has no sense of humor. Rabelais detested the *agélastes*. He feared them. He complained that the *agélastes* treated him so atrociously that he nearly stopped writing forever.

No peace is possible between the novelist and the *agélaste*. Never having heard God's laughter, the *agélastes* are convinced that the truth is obvious, that all men necessarily think the same thing, and that they themselves are exactly what they think they are. But it is precisely in losing the certainty of truth and the unanimous agreement of others that man becomes an individual. The novel is the imaginary paradise of individuals. It is the territory where no one possesses the truth, neither Anna nor Karenin, but where everyone has the right to be understood, both Anna and Karenin.

In the third book of *Gargantua and Pantagruel*, Panurge, the first great novelistic character that Europe beheld, is tormented by the question: Should he marry or not? He consults doctors, seers, professors, poets, philosophers, who each in turn quote Hippocrates, Aristotle, Homer, Heraclitus, Plato. But after all this enormous, erudite research, which takes up the whole book, Panurge still does not know whether he should marry or not. And we, the readers, do not know either—but on the other hand, we have explored from every possible angle the situation, as comical as it is elemental, of the person who does not know whether he should marry or not.

Rabelais' erudition, great as it was, has a meaning other than that of Descartes. The novel's wisdom is different from that of philosophy. The novel is born not of the theoretical spirit but of the spirit of humor. One of Europe's major failures is that it never understood the most European of the arts—the novel; neither its spirit, nor its great knowledge and discoveries, nor the autonomy of its history. The art inspired by God's laughter does not by nature serve ideological certitudes, it contradicts them. Like Penelope, it undoes each night the tapestry that the theologians, philosophers, and learned men have woven the day before.

Lately, it has become a habit to speak ill of the eighteenth century, to the point that we hear this cliché: The misery that is Russian totalitarianism comes straight out of Europe, particularly out of the atheist rationalism of the Enlightenment, its belief in all-powerful reason. I do not feel qualified to debate those who blame Voltaire for the gulag. But I do feel qualified to say: The eighteenth century is not only the century of Rousseau, of Voltaire, of Holbach; it is also (perhaps above all!) the age of Fielding, Sterne, Goethe, Laclos.

Of all that period's novels, it is Laurence Sterne's *Tristram Shandy* I love best. A curious novel. Sterne starts it by describing the night when Tristram was conceived, but he has barely begun to talk about that when another idea suddenly attracts him, and by free association that idea spurs him to some other thought, then a further anecdote, with one digression leading to another—and Tristram, the book's hero, is forgotten for a good hundred pages. This extravagant way of composing the novel might seem no more than a formal game. But in art, the form is always more than a form. Every novel, like it or not, offers some answer to the question: What is human existence, and wherein does its poetry lie? Sterne's contemporaries—Fielding, for instance—particularly savored the extraordinary charm of action and adventure. The answer we sense in Sterne's novel is a very different one: for him, the poetry lies not in the action but in the *interruption* of the action.

It may be that, indirectly, a grand dialogue took shape here between the novel and philosophy. Eighteenth-century rationalism is based on Leibniz's famous declaration: *Nihil est sine ratione*—there is nothing without its reason. Stimulated by that conviction, science energetically explores the *why* of everything, such that whatever exists seems explainable, thus predictable, calculable. The man who wants his life to have a meaning forgoes any action that hasn't its cause and its purpose. All biographies are written this way. Life is shown as a luminous trajectory of causes, effects, failures, and successes, and man, setting his impatient gaze on the causal chain of his actions, further accelerates his mad race toward death.

Against that reduction of the world to the causal succession of events, Sterne's novel, by its very form, affirms that poetry lies not in action but there where action stops; there where the bridge between a cause and an effect has collapsed and thought wanders off in sweet lazy liberty. The poetry of existence, says Sterne's novel, is in digression. It is in the incalculable. It is beyond causality. It is *sine ratione*, without reason. It is beyond Leibniz's statement.

Thus the spirit of an age cannot be judged exclusively by its ideas, its theoretical concepts, without considering its art, and particularly the novel. The nineteenth century invented the locomotive, and Hegel was convinced he had grasped the very spirit of universal history. But Flaubert discovered stupidity. I daresay that is the greatest discovery of a century so proud of its scientific thought.

Of course, even before Flaubert, people knew stupidity existed, but they understood it somewhat differently: it was considered a simple absence of knowledge, a defect correctable by education. In Flaubert's novels, stupidity is an inseparable dimension of human existence. It accompanies poor Emma throughout her days, to her bed of love and to her deathbed, over which two deadly *agélastes*, Homais and Bournisien, go on endlessly trading their inanities like a kind of funeral oration. But the most shocking, the most scandalous thing about Flaubert's vision of stupidity is this: Stupidity does not give way to science, technology, modernity, progress; on the contrary, it progresses right along with progress!

With a wicked passion, Flaubert used to collect the

stereotyped formulations that people around him enunciated in order to seem intelligent and up-to-date. He put them into a celebrated *Dictionnaire des idées reçues.* We can use this title to declare: Modern stupidity means not ignorance but the *nonthought of received ideas.* Flaubert's discovery is more important for the future of the world than the most startling ideas of Marx or Freud. For we could imagine the world without the class struggle or without psycho-analysis, but not without the irresistible flood of received ideas that—programmed into computers, propagated by the mass media—threaten soon to become a force that will crush all original and indi-vidual thought and thus will smother the very essence of the European culture of the Modern Era.

Some eighty years after Flaubert imagined his Emma Bovary, during the thirties of our own century, another great novelist, Hermann Broch, wrote that however heroically the modern novel may struggle against the tide of kitsch, it ends up being over-whelmed by it. The word "kitsch" describes the attitude of those who want to please the greatest number, at any cost. To please, one must confirm what everyone wants to hear, put oneself at the ser-vice of received ideas. Kitsch is the translation of the stupidity of received ideas into the language of beauty and feeling. It moves us to tears of compassion for ourselves, for the banality of what we think and feel. Today, fifty years later, Broch's remark is becom-ing truer still. Given the imperative necessity to please and thereby to gain the attention of the great-est number, the aesthetic of the mass media is inevitably that of kitsch; and as the mass media come to embrace and to infiltrate more and more of our life, kitsch becomes our everyday aesthetic and moral code. Up until recent times, modernism meant a nonconformist revolt against received ideas and kitsch. Today, modernity is fused with the enormous vitality of the mass media, and to be modern means a strenuous effort to be up-to-date, to conform, to conform even more thoroughly than the most conformist of all. Modernity has put on kitsch's clothing.

The *agélastes*, the nonthought of received ideas, and kitsch are one and the same, the three-headed enemy of the art born as the echo of God's laughter, the art that created the fascinating imaginative realm where no one owns the truth and everyone has the right to be understood. That imaginative realm of tolerance was born with modern Europe, it is the very image of Europe—or at least our dream of Europe, a dream many times betrayed but nonetheless strong enough to unite us all in the fraternity that stretches far beyond the little European continent. But we know that the world where the individual is respected (the imaginative world of the novel, and the real one of Europe) is fragile and perishable. On the horizon stand armies of *agélastes* watching our every move. And precisely in this time of undeclared and permanent war, and in this city with its dramatic and cruel destiny, I have determined to speak only of the novel. You may have understood that this is not some attempt on my part to avoid the questions considered grave. For if European culture seems under threat today, if the threat from within and without hangs over what is most precious about it—its respect for the individual, for his original thought, and for his right to an inviolable private life—then, I believe, that precious essence of the European spirit is being held safe as in a treasure chest inside the history of the novel, the wisdom of the novel. It is that wisdom of the novel I wanted to honor in this speech of thanks. But it is time for me to stop. I was forgetting that God laughs when he sees me thinking.